to Sfax

El Guettar

ITALIAN POSITION
THIS IS THE FUNNEL

OUR MINE FIELDS

to Gabes

RAILROADS
ROADS
0   1   2   3   4   5 Miles

THE BATTLE
IS THE PAY-OFF

by

RALPH INGERSOLL

HARCOURT, BRACE AND COMPANY   NEW YORK

This book is complete and unabridged.
It is manufactured in conformity with government regulations for saving paper.

Foreword

THE powers of careful observation and clear description of scenes and events have not been bestowed equally upon all of us; and but few of those so gifted or trained ever write of their experiences and observations.

Fortunately, Captain Ingersoll has those powers, and he has promptly written out what he so carefully observed. His description of the battle near El Guettar and the events both immediately before and after the battle make a living scene peopled by our own soldiers fighting against our principal enemies. It may be rather strong reading for some, but it must be remembered that a battle is not a game of ping-pong. It is a ferocious engagement and is met by thousands of our soldiers and of our allies every day in some part of the world.

Those at home and those who are about to enter a theater of operations—particularly the latter—will better do their part in this war if they realize more exactly what is going on at the final "business" end of the war structure. I do know, from my own experiences, that this is true for newly trained soldiers; and so I hope that some of them who may chance upon this book will read it carefully and benefit by the experiences described.

DANIEL NOCE,
Brigadier General, U. S. Army.

May 27, 1943

Author's Note

ALL the characters in the book are real persons. But since under the circumstances in which the book was written it was impossible to show them the manuscript, I have out of deference to them used fictitious names for everyone except a few general officers.

R. I.

Table of Contents

To
Geraldine

Introduction

WHEN I first went into the army I was very unhappy. I was not permitted to enter the army as an anonymous draftee, which would have given me a sense of community with millions of other Americans. The atmosphere of public controversy which surrounded me as editor of the newspaper *PM* penetrated into the circumstances connected with my joining the armed forces. I was a newspaper man and I thought and still do think that newspaper publishing is an essential war occupation. But, after all, no one can shed completely one's own personal bias in such matters. I had to solve the tangle in my own way, and recalling the first World War, when I enlisted in the army at the age of seventeen, I threw off my personal bias by enlisting again and shedding my prejudice in favor of fighting this war as publisher and editor. I ceased to be unhappy.

The process by which I ceased to be unhappy was the process of absorption into that vast community which is the Army of the United States. To each man this process is personal, intimate, and individual. Even if I could entirely explain it, the explanation would be out of place here.

In this book there is little, for instance, about what we are fighting for or about the political situation in Europe or even about what I think of the coming peace. These subjects are missing, not because I have lost interest in them—I am quite sure there is more thinking on what the war is all about in the army than in any other large group in our society— but because—well, I can put it best by going back to my thoughts and emotions in the first month or two of training.

I was then so tired physically that I could only get through a day by using every five- or ten-minute breathing spell to lie flat on my back and luxuriate in my aches and pains. My friends had just begun coming to see me and their misguided way of showing their sympathy was to be indignant about "the way I was treated." Since I was low and dispirited, when they went away I found myself agreeing with them. I became so sorry for myself that I knew I would have to do something about it.

And these thoughts came to me—alone and in bull sessions on the bunks in the barracks and in ten-minute breaks in the field, talking with other men who, each in his own way, were going through an emotional experience something like my own:

Forget draft boards and legal or moral compulsions. Take the world as it is today. How would each one of us act if we were completely free agents? Would we still go to war or would we sit this one out?

We had been soldiers now for a month. That's long enough to know how tough it is for a soft civilian to march even five miles with nothing but a rifle on his shoulders and no pack, how uncomfortable it is to sleep on a hard and narrow cot. It is long enough, too, to know that, man for man, in the field, soldiers who could walk not five but twenty miles and to whom a cot was not a hardship but a luxury, would have very little difficulty killing us.

The military phrase for a soldier's mission is quite explicit. It is to impose one's will on the enemy. At the end of a month in the army we knew—and it was quite a startling bit of new knowledge—how weak we were, how easy it would be in a showdown for anyone to impose his will on us. If we were not yet disciplined, we already knew the value of discipline—for already we had been lost on marches, we had mock-fired in mock skirmishes on those who were supposed to be our friends. We knew, all the big talk aside, how we stank.

We also knew, fresh in the morning, marching in solid columns, swinging out from camp with our new M-1's on our shoulders, just how tough an army that was good could be.

Well, the German army was that good—as good as we felt in the early morning, as good as the best of our daydreams about ourselves.

All right, so that's the German army and maybe the Japanese army too, and even the Italians must be better than we were. And there are all these armies in the world, our sworn enemies—our sworn enemies whether we were Republicans or Democrats, bright or stupid, skilled or unskilled.

So now, thinking it over, talking it over, what would we do—today—if there were no draft boards, no sudden impulses to enlist? Well, this was the choice that we now understood: that either we accepted the will imposed by armies made up of stronger, tougher, better soldiers than we, or else we—first individually and then collectively—would have to create an army that was even tougher.

Those of us who had been soldiers for a month now *knew* there was no middle ground whatever. There was no space left for political debate. With the first personal understanding of the power, the sheer physical might, of an organized army, you knew you either had to be submissive to the will of an enemy with such an army or else you had to help create an organization strong enough to oppose it.

And now it came home to each of us that the only way to create such an organization was by sweat. Thought alone would not produce an army, nor would resolutions, or trades previously mastered. The new trade of killing must be learned from the hard ground up. The complete absorption of each one of us was required, physical and mental.

All our faith was needed, too. Now that our turn had come, we did not know, any one of us, whether we would be up to the rôle that history was giving us. We knew we would not know until we met the men in German gray-green or Japanese light khaki on something we could as yet only imagine, something called a battlefield.

I said we used to talk about what we would do if we were free agents. Most of us felt, some of us knew, that we were still free to accept or reject the ultimate challenge. We were not really committed yet. Very few of us would ever fight. The army, we saw, was plenty big enough to carry any given individual or group of individuals who chose to remain non-combatant throughout the war. The combatant idea was not dependent upon whether one became an infantryman with an assignment to a combat regiment but on whether one accepted personally the challenge to submerge oneself into the army and live wholly to make it stronger. There would be men—we could already spot some of them in our midst—who were only in the army for the ride and would always be passengers.

These were the thoughts that I and many others had and talked about in the summer of 1942, in the training battalion of the 533rd Engineer Shore Regiment at Camp Edwards, Massachusetts. They frightened me because I did not know how it would come out with me and also because I wondered, looking about me, whether we as a nation, as a people, would understand the inexorability of the choice. Would enough of us choose to resist rather than to submit? Were we really committed?

It was painfully obvious to the most casual observer in the summer of 1942 that Americans did not then understand. The pace of the army's training, the controversies in the papers, the crowds at the USO, the ceaseless murmuring tide of talk, talk, talk, from one continental coast to the other, the silly nonsense on the advertising billboards, the bad taste of the speeches to raise money for war bonds—everywhere one turned, there were the symptoms. The whole American world seemed unconscious of what were the only realities to us in camp. The hardness of the ground when you threw yourself on it making mimic charges—that was real. The hard ground symbolized the truth that only the hardness and discipline and self-consecration of millions could produce an army that could impose its will on the enemy who was attempting to impose his will on us.

Aching on the ground, I thought of the softness of a bed. Hungry on the cook's bad day, I thought of the dinner that

I had the money to buy if I were somewhere else. And I understood the appeaser for the first time. The appeaser, I thought, was simply a more imaginative man than I. He was simply a man who could look ahead and see the price he would have to pay for opposing the will of the armed enemy. Feeling the softness of his bed and the cool caress of the sheets and the peace that comes only with the full belly, he knew he would be content to submit to the conqueror just to be allowed to stay where he was. He understood the bargain he was making; he was prepared to rely on his wits to see that the enemy lived up to his end of it. I understood how he felt and I wished sometimes that I felt the same way.

I remembered the old soldier's story about the private in Stonewall Jackson's army. The old private had marched his feet off. He was sore and hungry and miserable and barely able to keep up with the column, when Stonewall Jackson rode alongside and asked him how he felt. The old soldier trudged in silence for a moment, then he said soberly: "I'm all right, General. But God damn my soul if I ever love another country."

There in the training battalion I could go back over my whole life and everything I had loved and what had given me satisfaction and what had made me unhappy, uncomfortable, or depressed. On the one side of the ledger there was the way of life that was gone, but on the other there was everything else. There was love and work and faith and the hope for the future of man that alone makes the terror of the present livable. There was everything except physical comfort, which grew suddenly insignificant. There was no way back out of the army, or even into a soft job in the army. At forty-two years of age, I might never fire a rifle, but there was only one way, now that I was in the army, and that was towards becoming the best soldier—with all my long inventory of limitations—that the army and I could make of me.

With these thoughts, and with the gradual hardening of muscles and the acclimatization to or acceptance of the army, or whatever the process should be called, I ceased being unhappy. I also ceased being a journalist. I became one-four-millionth or one-seven-millionth or one-eight-millionth part of the Army of the United States—for the duration.

I do not yet feel I know the answer to how good an army we are or will be. I admit, however, to a faith in us I did not have when I was in training and which I acquired slowly and only after many doubts. We are still not as good an army as the Russian or the British or the Chinese—let alone the German. We are probably better now than the Italian. I have no first-hand knowledge of the Japanese. But anyone who has been in the army for nearly a year will have felt at one time or another what, coming back from Africa, I felt most strongly—that as an army we are alive and growing. We grow in strength and perception because we are young and healthy. And we are big physically and can lose much blood without our wounds being mortal—terrible as is the sight of that blood flowing away.

This book is written in that faith in the American army that I have just confessed. It is also written with love and admiration.

PART I

Theater of War

1

THE orders came at 5 o'clock in the afternoon.

I was sitting in the sun outside the battalion headquarters and I was bored.

Battalion headquarters were in the last of a row of one-story mud houses. In front of the houses was a row of withered and dusty trees. The lowest branches were just high enough to let the half-tracks get under them. The half-track crews had the guns out and were cleaning them on the ground. Long belts of ammunition hung down from the branches and the parts of several guns were laid out neatly on canvas shelter halves (pup tents) on the ground. The men were sitting cross-legged or were sprawled out, working on the guns with grease-blackened toothbrushes and bits of rag.

The houses and the trees were on the edge of the big square in Gafsa, right where the road from Feriana came into it and turned left. From there the road wound down through the town and across the wadi where the flood had wrecked the field kitchen and where the rusting skeleton of the drowned Italian tank still stood in the now dried river-bed. Beyond the wadi, the road curled between the mud walls that once enclosed the palm and olive groves. Most of the walls were flat now, trampled down by the engineers' big bulldozers to make way for the vehicles which had taken shelter in the precious shade beyond. All the olive and the palm groves in the oasis of Gafsa were now chockablock with vehicles. The mud which had mired them down after the rain of the week before had dried and turned to dust except in the deep hollows that were still chocolate-colored and full of cracks.

Beyond the groves that were full of men and machines, the road went out into the naked desert and forked north and east. And to the north and to the east the enemy waited.

Ten feet from where I lay, an MP in a white helmet stood directing traffic along this road. The traffic was inconsequential now. The armor had followed the infantry and now both divisions were on the far side of Gafsa, in the groves and scattered over the plains and deserts beyond.

The Free French had come and gone—from Lake Chad across the desert, some men said. They traveled in battered old tanks and lorries that looked as if they were falling apart. They were supposed to have gone on out to protect our right flank. Some of them were big, bearded men in greenish skirts which were pinned between their knees so that from one angle they looked as if they wore hobble skirts and from another pantaloons. Their rifles were very long. The dough-boys did not know how to take them and looked in silence when they marched or rode past.

The first few days had been a scramble. No one had had time to more than gape hurriedly, whether at the Free French or the ruins of the old fortress that had been blown up because there was an enemy ammunition dump in it, or even down the mysterious, twisting sidestreets of the Arab village. There was only time to pluck the lemons from the trees and drive on to find a place to bivouac or a site for a gun or a water-point or someone else's command post. All had been confusion and haste, for no one had known when the counterattack might come. Then finally there was a little order in the chaos. Men began to know who and what out-fits were where. And the wire was in and sometimes you could raise someone on the field telephone. And the blankets were almost dry.

The only sign of the enemy all this time was the sight of

the reconnaissance planes making their leisurely circuits of the skies, morning and afternoon. They flew haughtily past with all the countryside belching fire and smoke up at them, not even swerving from the path they had chosen for themselves.

On that afternoon, I sat in the sun and was bored because I wanted to be out with A company. A company was reconnoitering the site for another mine field. I enjoyed reconnoitering and all my friends were in A company. But instead of being with them, I was sitting there in front of the battalion headquarters because the colonel had sent for me but had been away when I got there—and that was now four hours ago. I was still sitting on my can and I was tired of watching the MP or the men cleaning the guns or the puppies that played in the dirt by the door. The headquarters inside was a table and a field telephone and a box full of papers that a discouraged-looking sergeant was wearily reading and sorting. The adjutant, who was a busy little captain, breezed in and out with an air of making work for himself. Now and then he paused to reassure me that the colonel would be back soon.

There was a first-class rumor around that afternoon. This rumor had it that having taken over Gafsa and "consolidated the position," we were going to be pulled out of the line and sent north. If you had not heard the rumor, you could have felt it in the way men moved, known it from the tone of their voices and from what they were doing. The Gafsa show was over. It had been a "dry run." On the rifle range, a dry run is a drill in loading and aiming with no shooting. It is a rehearsal, a sham, not the real thing. There had been no enemy in Gafsa to meet the attack that had been so carefully planned. The artillery had fired its barrage, the combat teams had gone forward on foot, the Rangers had scaled the big mountains to the south to take a gun position on the summit and the light bombers had gone over in sheets—with their bombs falling like wind-driven hail. But the only enemy counteraction had been a single, thunderous explosion when they blew up the road on the edge of town. It made a crater twenty feet deep. But the enemy left no men to guard the hole. The advancing column rolled down around the edge of it and on into the town, finally overtaking even the engineers with their mine detectors and the skirmish line. The attack had been a shadow boxer's haymaker—full of speed and power and landing on nothing. There weren't even any respectable booby traps in town—the too obvious one in the gasoline pump on the main street was typical.

The day after the attack, the rain that was supposed to have stopped for good two weeks before came again in a deluge, and the armored division and the motorized infantry division both played still pond—no more moving. Every vehicle that could carry more than half a ton seemed to be stuck fast up to its hubs. When the peeps, whose drivers don't believe any terrain can stop them, tried to ford the streams, as often as not they would be washed downstream, turned over, rolled and wrecked. Only the big caterpillar-tracked bulldozers could be sure of waddling safely through the ooze. For twenty-four hours the battle seemed to be with nature, to survive at all in the flood. The men grew good-natured after the tension of the advance and there was a lot of kidding. It was so damn wet. The only places where there was cover from the sky were in the groves, and in an oasis the groves, of course, are diked to hold the water in. The men were standing in the rain, soaked to the skin. There did not seem to be a dry blanket anywhere. Back of the plains, behind the village, the columns that were to have leap-frogged to attack beyond Gafsa had dispersed at nightfall. In the morning their vehicles were sunk so far down they thought they'd be there for the duration.

It had taken twenty-four hours of winching and towing, pulling and lifting, to get the columns back on the road and through the town and out into something resembling a defensive position, with guns unlimbered and pointed towards where the enemy must be. Then the rain had stopped and there had been wind and sunshine, and quicker than the eye

could follow it the swamp turned to desert again and our
working parties could get on with laying new mine fields.
The radio began to work again and the men to dig. And
now, that afternoon, the job was done and everyone relaxed
and knew that we were coming out of the line. *This* rumor
was hot. We would be out by tonight—or by tomorrow.

And then, instead, came the order to go into battle.

2

THE big battle orders are usually very formal documents. First, they tell everything there is to know about the enemy —what positions he holds and with what troops and weapons. Then one's own position is inventoried, after which comes a statement of one's own objectives—the mission of the army or the corps or the division as a whole. And finally there is the breakdown of this mission into the individual missions of individual units.

The writing is succinct, devoid of adjectives, full of initials and abbreviations.

To this central document, other documents, called annexes, are appended. The annexes go into the details the main orders have no time for.

From this central document, product of the highest headquarters, stem equally formal, equally standardized orders to the component parts of the whole, until every single unit on the field is nourished with information and directives, all skillfully synchronized.

That's the way it is in the book; that's the way they learn it at the Staff School at Fort Leavenworth. In the field, it is often a great deal more casual.

I have seen the battle orders that launched three divisions in one counterattack in Tunisia. There were three hundred words of badly typed manuscript which directed this regiment here, and that over yonder, and such and such a battery to move to the crest of a hill northwest of such and such a town. The hour at which the attack would begin was added almost as an afterthought. The general shook his head when he showed the orders to me. He said: "They would never let me get away with that at Leavenworth. I guess I would have been court-martialed if we hadn't won."

To company officers—second and first lieutenants and captains—battle orders usually come by word of mouth: "Take two half-tracks and go there. At H minus 30 do this. Be back at H minus 10 and jump off at H minus 5." The American army doesn't use the term zero hour in this war. The hour of the main attack is always referred to as the H hour. H minus 10 means 10 minutes before the main attack begins. H plus 1 hour is one hour after the main attack has begun. The H hour is always on D day. D plus 2 means two days later.

It was already D day when I sat in the sun, bored with waiting for the colonel.

The lieutenant colonel who commanded the engineer battalion was a tall, good-looking man in his thirties. He was up out of the peep and into the building before I could get to my feet. The adjutant and the captain of B company were in the doorway. And all the colonel had said as the door closed behind him was, "O.K., now this is the dope. . . ."

Yet, five minutes later when the colonel and the two captains came out—I swear it—every man on the square at Gafsa knew that the rumor that we were being pulled out was baloney, and that instead we were about to make an attack, and in a hell of a hurry. I knew it without knowing how I knew it. The sergeant in the orderly room knew it, for he was already stuffing the papers back into the box and reaching for the lid. The gunners around the half-track knew it, for they were looking at each other as if to say, "See, I could have told you so" and had already begun putting the guns together again.

Across the square you could see men knew it by the way they walked. Men in the army come to know many things without speech. The way the commanding officer gets out of a peep, the way his driver wheeled it in. Fear, confidence, anxiety, humor—emotions communicate themselves from man to man, ripple across the surface of a camp or a battlefield like breezes across the surface of a still pond.

The air that had been calm was now tense and nothing had happened except that a lieutenant colonel had walked rapidly into a building, followed by two of his captains. Out from under trees and from houses, other officers appeared. Sergeants left the men they were sitting or working with. They did not come up to the door of the headquarters. They simply moved to where they could watch the junior officers who were moving towards the door. Each man had his own plans for getting the information he knew he would need.

The colonel came out and I blocked his path so that he could not overlook me, for I was an extra officer and already I knew I could be lost in the shuffle. The colonel blinked at me from under his helmet. He had been thinking of other things. He was in motion again, with me at his side, when he said:

"D company is going out with the Rangers. I heard you wanted to go on a raid with them. Do you still want to go?"

"Yes, sir," I said, striding along.

"O.K., tell Captain Henry I said you are assigned to him for the action. He is to use you as a regular officer." Suddenly he stopped, and I stopped, and he spoke as if some afterthought had made him regret what he said. "Look here, are your feet all right? Are you in good shape?"

I said, "Yes, sir, I'm in good shape."

He said irritably, "Well, God damn it, keep your head down and keep your tail down, too. I don't want visiting officers shot around here." Then he was gone. As he went down the square, other officers swung alongside him and he spoke a few words to each. After each conference, he moved on impatiently.

To each officer to whom the colonel spoke, except me, came sergeants and staff sergeants and first sergeants, and all over the square there were little conferences. Men began running in and out of buildings and the motors of the trucks and peeps and half-tracks began to start and the whole square was alive and roared and hummed. Round the corner, where the MP still stood, the peeps and the command cars that had swung quietly past now raced. Their brakes screeched as they took the corner.

I did not know Captain Henry or where he was or any more about him than that he commanded a company that did not exist in the table of organization of an engineer battalion. Captain Henry's was called a provisional (i.e., experimental) heavy weapons company. A normal engineer battalion in a line division has three companies, so that one may work with each of the three regiments that make up the triangle of a triangular division. The mission of these combat engineers is "to facilitate the movement" of the division and to put in its water-points—that is, to provide it with drinkable water in sufficient quantities, wherever and however it may have to dig, pump, disinfect, or decontaminate what water it can find.

Each engineer company has certain weapons with which to defend its working parties. In the battalion I was with, all the heavy weapons of all three engineer companies had been segregated into an unorthodox D company. Thus D company became a pool of weapons from which the other companies might draw details when security was needed. Whenever, in the past week, we had gone out to lay mines beyond our lines, A company's commanding officer had stopped by headquarters and drawn a half-track or two from D company to watch over us while we were out there. It was the half-tracks' job to protect us from strafing planes and to keep us safe from any enemy patrols which might show up.

The half-track is a kind of mechanical centaur. The front part—the wheels, the motor and hood and the driver's seat— is truck. The back part is armored tractor. Instead of a set of rear wheels, there are rubber-tired caterpillar treads, and above them a five-by-ten-foot steel box, with sides about three feet high. This armored box can be used in emergencies as a truck but it is built to carry weapons. As our half-tracks were rigged, they mounted two .50-caliber machine guns on pedestals, fore and aft in the steel box. With their long black barrels, these guns looked like attenuated cannon. On either side, amidships of the steel box, were .30-caliber machine guns. All four guns could fire in any direction except down. That is, they could fire forward over the driver's compartment, or to the sides or rear, or into the air at diving planes.

A half-track was a commonly accepted talisman against dive bombers. It was understood that when recognized from the air they would not be attacked. So the half-tracks were usually posted in a conspicuous place on some rise of ground near the working parties, where they would have elbow room to shoot in all directions. They rested there like chips on the shoulders of our working parties, daring the Luftwaffe to knock them off.

D company—the engineers' provisional weapons company —had three of these fine contraptions. In addition, the company commander had talked some ordnance officer out of a battery of 81-mm. mortars. Mortars, 81 or 60 mm., are strictly not engineers' weapons. They are infantry weapons. Their presence, however, was not the only thing that was unorthodox about D company. D company had all the half-tracks and a battery of mortars too, and in addition two of its squads were called "hell squads."

These squads were of young men whose ambitions to be commandos had been frustrated. Instead of commandos, they found themselves only combat engineers. So, when volunteers for two special raiding squads were called for, these men had stepped forward. Special raiding squads are no more typical of engineers than mortars, but D company had them.

The men in the hell squads carried knives and some of them had brass knuckles. The mission I had somewhat timidly volunteered for earlier in the afternoon was typical of the kind of high jinks they liked. Their plan was to cut in between two enemy positions, in trucks if possible, and then to circle behind the enemy lines on foot to reach a road which led back towards where the enemy's reserves were thought to be. The hell squads were then to mine this road—and beat it. Presently our infantry, co-operating, would simulate an attack on the front line. The alarmed enemy outposts were then expected to call for reserves and up they would come, rushing over the newly mined road behind their own lines.

This project I had heard gossiped about earlier in the day and had asked the adjutant, if the colonel hadn't some urgent assignment for me, could I go along, maybe. The sudden orders for the whole division to attack had, I gathered, swept the hell squad project to one side. Instead, they and the rest of D company were to "go out" with the Rangers.

I had not the remotest idea what this meant and knew only vaguely that there were any Rangers in the vicinity. The Rangers are the American counterpart of the British Commandos. They are specially trained volunteers, organized in small groups and usually used for raids only—that is, to capture prisoners, to cause diversions, to harass and disturb the enemy's peace of mind. This was almost all I knew about the Rangers before I found myself attached to them.

When the engineers' colonel disappeared across the square, a variety of emotions swept in upon me. Somewhere deep down inside me a cold flame of fear was lit. This I had expected. Until the actual orders for battle come, every soldier knows that confidence in how he will feel is just so much bunk. Bombed I had been—aplenty—when I was a civilian. Frightened I had been often enough, and really terrified several times. But there was about the order to go into battle something that was already different from those experiences. An order to go into battle is an irrevocable commitment. It is a beginning of which one does not know the end. It is the thought behind the slang phrase "This is it."

When it begins, there is no time to think of these feelings. They are just there, lying in the pit of the stomach. Everything else is action. Standing alone in the square with the colonel disappearing, I had to find D company and then its Captain Henry and from him discover what he wanted of

me and when and where. I knew from the presence of the
half-tracks that D company's headquarters must be near.
A minute's watching the coming and going of officers and
men and I decided it was in the building at the far end of
the row which began with battalion headquarters.

The room I entered could have belonged only to D company. There were two cots and a table in it. Both cots and
the table and most of the floor were littered with weapons
and ammunition. There were boxes of yellow hand grenades,
tommy guns, clips of ammunition, accouterments and paraphernalia. Men were coming and going, stuffing ammunition
in belts, hunting through the mess for something they
wanted but could not find. A second lieutenant in his early
twenties, blond and with a round face, cleared a space on
one of the bunks and sat there wedging things into the
pockets of his field jacket.

In the army when things are happening you don't ask any
more questions than you need to. I leaned against the table
and waited for someone with a captain's insignia on his helmet to show up. In his own corps area, General Patton made
all officers paint their insignia on the front of their steel
helmets. The junior officers called their yellow and silver
bars "aiming stakes"—they thought of them as handy markers
by which enemy snipers could single them out.

Presently, a bustly little man with two unmistakable white
bars on his steel forehead popped in and was about to pop
out again when I nailed him. Before I could say, "Lieutenant
Ingersoll reporting," he said:

"Colonel Bentwood told me you were coming with us.
Look, this is how it is"—the lieutenant on the bunk pricked
up his ears—"Wait a minute"—to the lieutenant—"Get the
rest in here."

The lieutenant stuck his head around the doorway and
yelled sergeant something. Presently several men and another
lieutenant crowded in. The captain shoved his helmet on the
back of his head and said rapidly:

"The other business is off." He meant the raid. "We're

going out with the Ranger battalion. No half-tracks. The half-track squads are to take the mortars. I want the hell squads first. We'll go out in trucks. This is the timetable. At 8:45 we have to pick up the mines in front of the Rangers' outpost on the Sfax road. They are in both forks on the road. Get whoever put them in, and you"—pointing to one of the lieutenants—"go up and get that done while the rest of you wait just back of the Rangers' post. You are to be all through with the mines in an hour and come back. At 11:45 we take off with the Rangers." He looked at his watch. "It is 20 minutes past 5 now. We don't need to be ready until about 7:30 or 8. Tell the men to get set and then take it easy. I want everybody except the half-track drivers. Load all the junk we'll leave behind in the half-tracks. Get the kitchen packed up and we can send back for the stuff when we need it. Take enough food with you for thirty-six hours."

Nobody said anything during this speech or after it. There were no questions. The captain then said:

"I've got to get hold of somebody and find out where the hell the Rangers want us. Exactly, I mean."

Then—"Oh, yes," pointing suddenly to me, "this is Lieutenant Ingersoll. He's coming with us. You two"—to the second lieutenants—"take the platoons and Ingersoll will come with me. And for Christ's sake will you all keep together."

And then he, too, was gone.

It was 5:20 and the show wasn't to begin until well after 7. The men drifted out and the buzz subsided a little.

I thought to myself, "Thirty-six hours is a long time. It is going to raise the question of whether I *can* take it physically. The thing for me to do for the next two hours is rest because I expect there will come a time when whether I am physically able to walk another mile or two is going to make a difference."

I was quite right.

3

I SAT on the bunk in D company's storeroom and tried to relax. Men came and went, checking their equipment, stopping to work the mechanisms of their weapons, counting ammunition, changing their boots. Through the window across the room I could look out onto the square where there was continual movement—dust and men and machines—without pattern.

I thought, "I would rather go into action with A company than with these men in D company whom I don't know." I felt that A company was "my outfit" even though I had served with it for no more than a week. A single week, but the days had been long and full of experience. At night I had been one of the family with the young officers and the talk had been easy and intimate. I had arrived the first morning in Gafsa with the rain. All the experiences of the last weeks came back to me as I sat waiting and I re-lived them. Because now that I was going out with the division life seemed to date from when I left Algiers to join it.

In Algiers my orders had simply been to proceed to headquarters of the Second Corps of the American Army, and there to get further orders assigning me to whatever engineer battalion was in the line. I was being sent up to "get experience"—and to study mine-removal technique.

An Army Corps is technically but a part of an army. Two or more divisions make a corps and two or more corps make an army. But the four American divisions that composed the

Second Corps in Tunisia were then already functioning as a field army, responsible neither to the Eighth Army on the south nor the First Army to the north. On that date, the Eighth Army was still on the other side of the Mareth Line. The American Second Corps was an autonomous field organization responsible only and directly to Generals Alexander and Eisenhower at Allied Forces Headquarters.

At home, headquarters are listed in the telephone book and anyone can direct you to them. In the field, the whereabouts of headquarters are important military secrets. The adjutant who issued me my orders in Algiers could not tell me where I would find the Second Corps headquarters at the front. Under some persuasion, he named me a town where I might inquire. This turned out to be 100 miles off base. So I lost a day in a false start.

The hub city of the Tunisian front was Constantine, high in the mountains due east of Algiers, halfway to the front. From America, the convoys came to Casablanca and Rabat on the Atlantic and to Oran and Algiers on the Mediterranean. From these ports supplies went forward in endless convoys of trucks, crawled up the winding railroads with so many different gauges—there were four or five different widths of tracks in Africa—or crept along the shore line in little coasters to the bombed, harassed, and overworked little ports of Phillipville and Bone. From these ports, most supplies found their way by road and rail to join the other streams at Constantine. All across Africa I had watched the life blood of the army pumping steadily through these arteries, all day and all night, never stopping. It was an inspiring sight.

Constantine itself was set near the very top of a chain of jagged peaks. A thousand-foot gorge splits the ancient city, arched over with bridges that hold one half of the city to the other. The airports which Constantine had to use were some miles out, beyond where the mountains fell away into foothills and flattened into plains. One of these airports was called Tellergma.

Between Algiers and Tellergma, courier planes shuttled back and forth almost hourly. They rose up out of the airport at Algiers and climbed hard to clear the first passes of the mountains, which have snow on them. It was a wild two-hour ride, looking up at the top of the mountains as the plane lurched through the twisted air in the valleys.

When I rode up on a plane in the early afternoon I felt as if I were leaving all the world I had known. When one moves to join an army that is actually fighting in the line, one crosses a very real frontier. One moves from the world where all is talk and theory and enters the world where only the reality of action counts.

The courier planes at the front are as alike as peas. They are the familiar DC-3's of the American commercial lines, painted olive drab. Inside, instead of reclining chairs, they have what are known as bucket seats. These are long, continuous shelves of aluminum with scalloped seats stamped in them. These shelves run down either side of the plane. In the center the luggage is piled, bedding rolls and barrack bags, musette bags and a few officers' suitcases. In the rear of the plane, there is another great pile of luggage with usually a rifle or two or a tommy gun leaning against it. The loading is casual and the baggage is not weighed; you throw your stuff in and you climb aboard.

On that first flight up, with a new steel helmet on my head for the first time and a .45 pistol and three clips of ammunition and a canteen on the belt around my trenchcoat, I looked more like a soldier than I felt. Now that I was on my way I thought, as each civilian turned soldier must one time think, of the shabbiness of my coat of training. You feel as if nearly a year's training were no more than a thin paint which is already wearing off and letting the original color show through. The uniform feels like a fancy-dress costume, something hired and unreal. You are there under false pretenses. You are not a soldier at all but simply someone dressed up to look like a soldier.

The boy on the bucket seat next to me was a young cor-

as the men opened their letters and read by its uneven light. Six or eight sacks of mail had come up on the plane with me.

From Canrobert I got a ride sixty kilometers back into Constantine and there, since I was an engineer, I sought out the engineers' headquarters. The engineers were in Nissen huts—the round, galvanized iron huts the British use. They were dug into a hillside in a grove of pine trees. It was quiet and orderly there and everyone was very busy working to keep the stuff moving through Constantine to the front. When I showed my orders, the adjutant there told me where to go next, and in the afternoon one of the colonels sent me on my way.

4

BEYOND Constantine, the names of units were in code. The Second Corps headquarters was known as Ready. In the forward zone, headquarters of any size are split in two. One is called the forward headquarters, the other the rear. Ready Rear was where I would find the next adjutant and I went up in a jeep driven by a sergeant. The colonel put me in charge of his cargo: a fine fresh side of beef he was sending up as a present to the First Armored Division's mess.

"If they stop you," said the colonel, "the beef is nobody's business. You're to get the sergeant through to Tebessa where he will drop you off. Ready Rear is somewhere around there. I couldn't tell you quite where. The sergeant's got to go on to the Kasserine Pass."

The colonel had been standing by the motor pool under the trees. "Holy smoke," he said, "let me look at you. Give me that helmet. Here, McCloskey, get some paint."

My unscarred helmet had no insignia on it.

"There's a fine for that in Patton's area," the colonel said. Then he looked me over again, pointing to the various articles. "It's $25 if you haven't your pistol belt on and $10 for no tie and $15 if you leave your leggings off. He's got a special detail to report officers. That's a great crew—those fellows in the First Armored. The sergeant here used to be with them. See that they get their beef."

McCloskey gave me my helmet back with its new bar of white paint still wet, and off we went.

Tebessa was something over a hundred miles of macadam road away. Constantine was the hub of the whole Tunisian supply system; Tebessa was where the dumps were. Tebessa was the big treasure chest into which two armies dipped for food and ammunition, gasoline, and a thousand miscellaneous supplies. Later on, when the Eighth Army smashed through the Mareth Line, the world heard about the dumps of Tebessa. General Eisenhower made a point of them in his review of the campaign. The Eighth Army had left its supplies behind when it cracked the Mareth Line. It raced north with what it could carry. The wall of French and American troops that flanked the coastal plain was to guard the dumps at Tebessa until the Eighth Army, joining up, could get at them.

But I knew none of this as we rocked and twisted in and out of the gutter, off the road and on, from Constantine to Tebessa, past streams of convoys going up and coming back. The sergeant was not talkative. He was very busy. So was I, hanging on. We came at dusk across a plain and a rise of ground and there was the ancient walled city with its triumphal Roman arch looking out into the dusk.

In the last hour the sergeant had shown signs of nervousness. He was afraid I would take him out of his way to find the headquarters I was looking for. Sergeants have to handle lieutenants. He said he did not like going through the Kasserine Pass in the dark. He stopped pointedly by an MP on the corner so I told him to let me out there. When I was on the ground, the MP looked our vehicle over. He said, "That thing you've got in the back is dripping blood." The sergeant snarled at him. "Let it drip. It's for the First Armored and they've bled plenty." Then he was off.

With each mile I went toward the front, the shadow of the American defeat at Kasserine Pass, when the Germans came through and the whole American line for fifty miles to the south had had to swing back, seemed to loom larger. Beyond the pass at Kasserine, the Germans had been stopped. Now the American army was going back through the hills it had been driven from. But everyone at the front was still talking about Kasserine Pass and arguing about how it had happened and telling each other their own experiences there or at that time. And the dumps at Tebessa were what everyone had been most frightened of losing.

I saw them the next morning, when I went on up—square mile upon square mile of piles of stuff, spaced out in rows, dispersed as far as the eye could see. The field was so deep that it took an hour's fast driving to get from one end to the other. Here the yellow-banded ammunition, here the stacks of gasoline tins. Beyond, the food under tarpaulins. There was little camouflage. The distance between the piles was their only defense, that and the enormous size of the field— no string of bombs would have eaten more than a flea's bite from the great expanse.

West of Tebessa we passed a big fighter field. It was crouched down below the unfriendly skies with only the tops of tents that were dug in the ground showing. The tiny planes looked forlorn and abandoned and there was no sign of life around them. Everything but the planes was underground and the camouflage was as careful there as it was casual at the dumps.

At Tebessa I spent the night with the MP's. They did not like anyone to go on at night except with a patrol. The MP's put me up in the one-time civil prison that was now their barracks—put me up by kicking a space on the floor clear, where I undid my bedding roll and stretched out. The MP's mess was in a boxcar on a railway siding. After he got the gasoline stove to work, the cook made good wheatcakes in the morning.

In the rear echelon of the corps headquarters, there was only paper work. The headquarters was in tents on a sandy hill under a grove of scrub pine. The inside of the tents were brightly lit by electric lights. The electricity came from a generator truck that hummed nearby. The tents were noisy with the clacking of typewriters, full of tables and chairs and files, and the clerks were jammed together. The major was in a bad humor and said:

"This is an army and they give us about enough men to look after a division. And we are too far back. It takes three hours to get up to Forward."

The papers they were working on in the adjutant's tent were the records of casualties. They were trying to keep straight the names of the men who had been killed and where the bodies were—and what had become of the wounded. They were working very hard at it. Someone, however, apparently didn't think they were working hard enough. I remembered a general's telling me in Algiers that he had told his personnel officer that he could take only one boxful of the division's records when they sailed for Africa—and what he could do with the rest of the records if he did not want to leave them behind in England. I did not envy the conscientious officers and men of the adjutant's section.

"And now," said the major in Ready Rear, "we not only have all this work to do but we've got to keep our Goddamned helmets on all the time we are doing it! It's a new rule."

I stayed for noon chow at Ready Rear and went on soon after. The other guest in the mess tent that noon was a second lieutenant with a story. I watched him come up just before noon—in a peep with the top down and the windshield flat and a raincoat lashed across the glass pane of the windshield to keep it from reflecting light into the sky. The driver and the other enlisted man with the lieutenant both had long, shaggy beards. Each had a tommy gun slung over his shoulder and there were extra rifles in the back of the peep next to the lieutenant. The lieutenant was about twenty-five, sunburnt and solid.

Everyone in Ready Rear knew him because he came in to tell his story and make his request every three or four weeks. The story was a little better each time—not because he told it better but because more had happened. The request was always the same. He was the executive officer of the only American company of light tanks in action in Africa and his request was: Would, could somebody please do something, anything, about getting his company back with the American army? It had been attached to the French at the beginning of the campaign and long ago its records had been mislaid. Or so its officers thought. It got neither mail nor orders; it drew neither pay nor supplies—and it ate French food. It was the French food that the Americans did not like. The officers at Ready Rear were interested in the lost tank company, and I gathered that whenever the lieutenant showed up someone wrote another letter to someone, asking if anything could be done—but nothing ever was. Meanwhile, the story got better and better.

The American light tanks had made ten attacks and every fourth man in the little company had been decorated by the French government. It was all the Frenchmen could do to show their appreciation. The Americans had been fighting German Mark IV's and, lately, some 60-ton Mark VI's. The solemn, sunburnt lieutenant shook his head between mouthfuls and said:

"It's discouraging. The fellows are awful good shots but when they make direct hits the shells just bounce off."

The American light tank is armed with a 37-mm. gun. Cannon shell from German Mark IV's or VI's do not bounce off when they hit the armor plate of a light tank. So the officers at the mess asked the lieutenant what he did about it, anyway.

He said, "Oh, there's always something you can do about it but it's discouraging. You can hide most of the tanks and if the Mark IV's will chase the others you can get in behind and blow up a few trucks before you have to beat it."

And then he cheered up and said brightly, "We got a Mark VI last week."

"How did you do it?" I asked.

"Well," he said, "we tried running like hell when they chased us and dropping anti-tank mines behind us as we ran. We tried dropping them off in bunches. One of those big bastards ran on three mines all at once and it blew off a tread. Then we sneaked around the other side and kept popping at it until it went up."

The American company had lost about one fourth of its tanks. The others, we gathered, were kept running by sheer ingenuity and spare parts salvaged on the battlefield.

The month before, the Germans had apparently decided to end the nuisance of the American light tanks once and for all. They had wedged and chivied and herded the Americans down into a narrow valley. There the Americans had a little Arab village to hide in but the German tanks were all around them now and could sit out of range and blow up the village, house by house.

"And, by God," said the lieutenant, "what do you suppose happened then?" He gesticulated with a fork. "It was just like a wild west movie. Just exactly. There was a road from east to west across one end of the valley and that afternoon the whole damned First Armored Division of the United States army came up that road. Just as pretty as you please. Just like the marines rescuing the ranchers from the Indians. By God, sir, we didn't know they were coming and they didn't know we were there and the Germans didn't know they were coming, either. We would like to have gone along with them," he said ruefully, "but after they went by, we had to go back to that French chow."

"You know," he said to the colonel, "the French are all right, sir, but the men have eaten a lot of that French chow. They don't like it, sir, they just don't like it."

The colonel asked how far away the lieutenant's tanks were now. The lieutenant said about eighty miles.

"Have you got any trucks left?" the colonel asked.

The lieutenant said he had one 2½-ton truck that could still run.

"Well, look here," said the colonel, "you send it down here once a week and we'll fill it up with grub and you can eat C rations for a few days anyway."

"You haven't had any word from Algiers?" asked the lieutenant.

The colonel said no, he hadn't.

After mess, the lieutenant went over to his peep. His bearded drivers, who had been asleep in the shade, got up and the three of them drove off again—to go on fighting their own battles and burying their own dead and eating French chow except when they could get the 2½-ton truck through to Ready Rear for some C rations.

I left soon afterward. The colonel, who had to go up to Ready Forward, took me along. It was a harsh cold afternoon and I was glad the colonel had left the top up. In another peep that had gone forward, the officer had had an argument with the driver about that and made him put the top down so that he could watch for planes. I had seen no enemy planes so far and I thought the chances of their bombing a lone peep were pretty slim.

When we came over the pass beyond Tebessa, however, I could not believe we would not be attacked. For the road there, which had been winding through high, narrow mountain passes, suddenly swung down the face of a slope so steep as to be almost a cliff and below there lay a desert plain as flat as a plastered wall. Across that plain the road cut a sharp, straight line, and on the road—bumper to bumper, it seemed —were two solid lines of traffic, almost motionless. Yet there were no planes whatever in the sky. No patrol of guardian angels—nor any enemy, yet.

We crawled down the cliff and as we went, we could make out, one by one, the gun positions defending the pass. There were a great many guns there and a great many men were busy digging them in still deeper, camouflaging them with nets and the branches of trees and covering the shelter tents around them with dirt and stones. The guns were sighted down the road and at each twist, when I looked back, I looked into the muzzle of one. Along the sides of the road there was barbed wire, very neatly strung in the geometrical patterns shown in the field manuals. At intervals there were pill boxes made of sandbags and piled stone, with slits in them facing out over the plain. They were doing a lot of work on this position.

The colonel chuckled, nodding at all this activity. "They got a workout here. The Germans came to just the other end of that plain.

"I was grinning," he said, "because just back beyond, there used to be a replacement training center."

A replacement training center is a pool from which replacements are drawn by outfits in the line—replacements for casualties. It is a kind of a bull pen where new players are warmed up for the game.

"That replacement center there," said the colonel, "made military history. It's the only replacement training center in history that ever had to retreat under fire. They moved it back in a hell of a hurry when the Germans were down on the plain there. They felt it wouldn't be fair to trainees to let them get captured before they joined their outfits."

As we passed it, we could see no signs of the high-water mark of the German tide. All we could see was the still-desolate landscape, alternating between table-flat desert plains and sharp-sided mountains that rose straight up without even foothills to introduce them. The geography seemed to have no pattern, for these hills did not run east and west or north and south or even in chains. The ground was hard and rocky and only occasionally were there woods of scrub pine. On the otherwise treeless desert, there were occasional dips where the water came closer to the surface forming an oasis with something green growing in it.

Towns were far apart, and whereas back near Canrobert and Constantine the streets had been crowded with Arabs in soiled, white robes, and the shops were open and the carts in front of them piled with oranges, and old men sat on rickety chairs in sidewalk cafés or on the sidewalk itself in rows, their backs against the buildings—whereas there was all this to the rear, beyond Tebessa there were only soldiers in the streets and an occasional Arab who didn't look at ease, but hurried on as if expecting an MP to prod him with a gun.

Ready Forward was then in a town called Feriana. At home a town of the same size would have a post office and one general store. Feriana had a little square, with a Roman column in its center, surrounded by a group of one- and two-story buildings. From their symmetry, they must have housed a school or some government activity.

Feriana was conspicuous by the absence of any sign of life. The little group of buildings around the Roman column was hemmed in with barbed wire. Near its gateway stood not one but three MP's. They were the only tipoff. There were no vehicles parked, no motor pool, no messengers coming and going.

The colonel and I were hardly out of the peep before one of the MP's sent it on its way—"We'll call it for you when you need it, sir." This was the model discipline of the headquarters where General Patton ruled the roost. To an enemy plane, Feriana must look like any other deserted village near the front. The movement of vehicles must be scarce and unhurried. The intelligence would come in and the orders would go out by stealth or by wire.

When I left Algiers, the talk had been of supplies, not of fighting. There had not even been rumors of an offensive, at least within the next few weeks. There had been neither sight nor sound of action in Ready Rear, only the shuffling of the papers of the dead and disabled. There was still no sign in the deserted streets of Feriana. But when the colonel and I crossed the courtyard and stepped into the low-ceilinged hall of the central building, there it was—a fact accomplished.

It was like stepping in from a peaceful street to the tense stillness of an operating room. The surgeons and the consulting doctors were all there. Pacing back and forth in front of the little fireplace there was a man I recognized as General Alexander. Beyond him, General Eisenhower stood with his hands behind his back. General Patton was talking in whispers to a colonel who was very attentive and nodding his head. Except for the attentive colonel, I could not see a man in the room who didn't have stars on his helmet or the crossed sword and scabbard the British generals wear on their shoulders. It was suddenly like a wash drawing in *The Illustrated London News*, "The Generals Conferring in their Headquarters at the Front." Only they were not conferring. Except for Patton they were not saying anything. They were just looking like worried doctors waiting on the health of some patient who was very important to them. They were waiting for him to come out of the ether.

On either side of the room we had entered, through low doorways, we could see other rooms and in them officers, standing or sitting at tables, not saying anything. There were no couriers, no telephones. On the far wall of one room, I could see a big battle map with red and blue crayon marks on it. The marks were the little squares and crosses, dots and circles, initials and numbers that showed where the enemy were and where we were. No one was looking at it.

The colonel I had come with was there to pay a routine call. He was as appalled at where he found himself as I was. We looked at each other and knew that both of us felt as if we were intruders upon some family crisis of great delicacy. Something was happening, something these men had set in motion. From their faces you could not tell whether it was happening successfully or disastrously. You only knew that, having set it in motion, they could now do nothing about it.

The colonel and I moved on into the least crowded of the rooms on either side. The colonel had to find some junior officer; I was looking for a man known as the corps engineer. He was to forward me to my battalion. In the room we entered—it was the one with the map in it—there were two sergeants. One of them was looking at the keys of his typewriter, the other was reading a detective story. The one at the typewriter told me that the corps engineer was in the building to the left, just outside. I nodded to the colonel and tiptoed out, past the thoughtful generals. I crossed the courtyard and entered the door on which two words were written in small letters: Engineers—Artillery.

There were no generals inside this room but the atmosphere was exactly the same as in the headquarters. This was a big room with an arched ceiling. Its windows were blacked out but it was brightly lit from half a dozen hanging electric fixtures. It was filled with flat-topped desks and tables and at each sat an officer or an enlisted man—fifteen or twenty in all, and no one saying anything. Neither were they working. They were just looking at nothing and waiting.

A young man in a buttoned-up field jacket sat on the right side of the room near the door and on his desk a card proclaimed Lieutenant Smithers, C.E. C.E. means Corps of Engineers. He could not see the insignia under my trenchcoat, so I said to him, "I am an engineer officer and I am looking for the corps engineer." He looked up slowly, as if my presence brought him back to reality from some dream, and said:

"He is not in here. He is up with them, now. I am his assistant."

Then, as he saw the expression on my face, "They are going into Gafsa right now, you know. They took off this morning. We haven't heard anything here. Nobody tells us anything here. We're just waiting. Is it raining out?"

Thus it was that I came to where the battle began.

5

FERIANA is only forty miles from Gafsa—forty miles of desert, at the far end of which the ground suddenly uptilts into a mountain barrier cut through by a gaping pass beyond which is the oasis of Gafsa itself. Still farther beyond, you reach the chain of mountains and passes that lead to the coastal plains.

The action into which I had stumbled was the occupation of Gafsa by the First Infantry Division, the First Armored Division supporting. Across the wide flat plain these two divisions had crept, bringing up the guns and the ammunition, the vehicles and the supplies they would need for the attack. The gap was a natural defensive post for the enemy; the attack was mounted in force. On the morning of the day I came to headquarters it had taken off.

Even the next morning there was still no real news except that "we" were in Gafsa. Where was the enemy? They had not fired a shot. Early in the morning, the corps engineer, who is a colonel, had come back from the front. But he could tell us nothing except that it had begun to rain in the night. He doubted if the divisions could make the second day's objectives in the rain. It was the First Infantry Division that had occupied Gafsa. The First Armored's mission was now to scurry through the gap that had been cleared and to attack beyond.

Both the colonel and the lieutenant of engineers were preoccupied with the mine fields "we" had found around Gafsa.

On the wall back of the lieutenant's desk was a big six-foot-square map showing where our own fields were. Now the new enemy fields that had been located must be marked. The engineers attached to the corps headquarters do not do the locating and lifting. They keep the score, they co-ordinate efforts, and they advise the commanding general.

Sometime during the night, Lieutenant Smithers had heard of an Arab who claimed to have been in Gafsa the week before and said he had watched the enemy put in the mine fields there. When after breakfast his search was successful, Smithers came riding up to headquarters with the excited Arab in the back of his peep. He agreed to take me on into Gafsa, along with the Arab.

Now, but not until now, it was revealed that I was to be assigned to the First Engineer Battalion—the combat engineers with the First Infantry Division, General Terry Allen commanding, with General Teddy Roosevelt his assistant division commander.

The rain that was a drizzle at dawn was a cloudburst by 8 A.M. I had only my light trenchcoat to keep me dry. I had slept in an empty house across the road from headquarters and running back into it to be sure that I had left nothing behind I stumbled over a pile of trash. Kicking it absently I saw two pairs of oilskin pants. "I don't know whom these belong to," I said to myself, "but one of them can serve its country better on my legs than here." The oilskin pants were fine. Throughout the day they kept a whole two or three feet of me almost dry—a belt running roughly from a little below my waist to just above the knees. Throughout this protected zone, I was never more than damp.

The road from Feriana on was as empty the day after the advance as the road to Feriana had been crowded the day before. We met only rain and water sluicing across it, rain so heavy that the driver could not see a tank's length ahead, water inches deep. In the rain, the battle scars on the countryside seemed old enough to have been inherited from another war. The vehicles that lay burned and wrecked were already rusted. Where the railway ran parallel with the road and the bridges had been blown, the right of way seemed to have been abandoned for years. Dented and rusty cans were scattered on either side of the road and surface water was coming up around them.

Surface water turns the soil of the Tunisian plains from gray to dark brown. Every few miles the road dipped to ford a wadi that had been dry yesterday but today roared like a mountain stream. In each, as we came to it, the water was deeper than in the last. Now, as we crept through, clouds of steam went up as the water rose and touched our peep's hot exhaust pipe.

The first real sign of what had yesterday been the front line were the little placards stuck up on stakes on either side of the road, half red and half white but without lettering. They told in this design that to the right, beyond there, there was a mine field, to the left, there, from here to here, there was another. Then we began to bump through the craters from which the enemy's mines in the road had been removed —round holes, eighteen inches across and ten or twelve inches deep. They were partially filled in now. The holes would come in bands fifteen or twenty yards deep. When you went across them, if you looked at the side of the road, you could see piles of black metal pancakes. The pancakes were the Teller mines that had been taken up from the road. The mines in the desert on either side of the road were still in the ground.

Beyond the piles of Teller mines—you had to look sharp, going through the rain—you could see smaller piles of short, thick, black pencils. These were the activators for the Teller mines. The engineers had unscrewed them to make the mines safe to handle.

The evening before, and that morning at mess, I had talked mines with Lieutenant Smithers, filling in my book learning with his first-hand knowledge. Lieutenant Smithers was very sensitive to booby traps because, as he said, "It's always Corps that finds the booby traps that Battalion has overlooked."

What he meant was that when the combat engineers in the line, whose job it was to locate and clear the mine fields, missed a mine it stayed alive in the ground until the rear echelon moved up—the headquarters and the supply trains and all the paraphernalia of the corps. Sooner or later the men and the machines of Corps would run over or trample down every square foot of ground within miles. In running over and trampling down every square foot, Corps would inevitably explode every enemy mine that had been over-looked. And every time that happened, Corps had one, two, three, or four more casualties and, usually, one less vehicle.

All the stories of all the ingenious booby traps and all the freak mine accidents up and down the line came into, and cleared through, the corps engineer headquarters. Talking about mines with Lieutenant Smithers was like talking to an insurance salesman about accidents—an insurance agent who was really interested in the myriad risks there are in life. And, presently, like a prospective purchaser hearing an insurance agent inventory the risks, the listener, too, became sensitized. By the time we got to Gafsa, as far as I was concerned there were live mines under every cobblestone, and every doorway was a booby trap. I said as much to Smithers. He looked gloomily at me and said morosely, "Well, keep feeling that way. Maybe if you do you will get home whole."

6

THE formality of reporting at the front is brief. I had a lieutenant colonel to find, that first morning in the rain, and I ran him down a few miles beyond Gafsa. Most of the battalions and companies that had headquarters in town had stuck their little yellow fabric markers out on the road and if you could read the cryptic markings on them, and were patient and asked questions of passing soldiers, you could find your way around.

I left Smithers and his Arab in the rain-swept and deserted square and he lent me his peep to go on. Presently I found a dispatch rider sitting on his motorcycle with his feet in two mud puddles. He sat near a sign which indicated a battalion command post nearby. He answered my query:

"That's Colonel Bentwood, there," pointing to a command car which was lurching across the dikes of an olive grove beyond.

A helmeted head with a silver leaf on it came out of the side curtain and I gestured. Somewhere inside my soaking clothes was a paper but I simply shouted, "I'm reporting for duty, sir—I'm an observer officer—I'm from Allied Force Headquarters."

He yelled back, "See if you can find a young fellow named Lieutenant Cobb. He's A company. Stick with him and I'll send for you when we get settled."

The road outside was full of the motion of a division coming to rest in its bivouac area. They were laying telephone wire and it was unwinding from big drums on ¾-ton trucks. Jeeps and command cars were going by in both directions, some with harassed officers hanging on, standing on the running boards, peering into the mist for lost vehicles. A caterpillar bulldozer was trying to get a big tank destroyer out of the ditch. Doughboys stood about or walked past, water running off their helmets. They all carried rifles, some slung over their shoulders, butts up against the rain, others with rags stuffed in the muzzles to keep the water out or with bits of oilskin wrapped around the bolt mechanism. Everywhere on the road was bustle and confusion and the water in the ditches seemed to get deeper by the minute.

When my driver and I, seeking A company, came to the big wadi, we reached it just as the kitchen truck went off the edge of the concrete road. The concrete road was somewhere down under the muddy water. You could see there was nothing that could be done about the kitchen truck until the water went down but groups of men stood on the shore a few feet away looking thoughtful, groping for ideas. The white-helmeted MP's passed vehicles across the ford—a good city block long—one by one. Upstream, there were several jeeps and a ¾-ton truck bogged down with water running over the floor boards. They must have been looking for a shallower crossing. The peep I was in could take the water up to just below the brake pedal—an inch or two over the floor. We splashed through, and half a mile beyond we reached my destination.

Lieutenant Cobb was easy to find. He sat in the center of a clearing on the edges of which I could distinguish four or five 2½-ton trucks with their tarpaulin tops up, and a covered kitchen truck in which the cooks were working over a range. Round the edges of the clearing there were some tents made of shelter halves but in most of them the water was several inches deep. The men were simply standing about, leaning against the trees or the fenders of the trucks. Lieutenant Cobb sat on a gasoline tin, a raincoat strapped tightly around his neck, helmetless. Over him bent an enlisted man with a pair of shears. He was cutting off wet hand-fuls of the lieutenant's hair.

The lieutenant reached out from under the raincoat to shake hands, and said: "Hope you don't mind if I get this finished," pointing upward. "We may have to go out in a minute. Everything is to hell and bogged down. I've got one squad on the Maknassy Road looking for mines But, what the hell, it's too wet. I'll bet the detectors are rained out by now. I've got another squad trying to fix a washout in one of the wadis. The rest are digging stuff out of the mud. We'll go have a look in a while."

I stood in the mud and rain while the haircut progressed, because there was no place else to go and nothing to do but to stand there and get wetter.

7

MY first days in the line were long and lived casually. As an observer attached to A company of the First Engineer Battalion, I came and went almost as I pleased, going out first with one working party and then another. As soon as I came to know the terrain and where our troops were and what they were doing, I began picking up odd jobs for myself. When we had been out on a reconnaissance with the C.O., I would be sent back with the information we picked up and told to bring a platoon out to where some work had to be done.

Engineers at home may do anything from designing a flood spillway on the Mississippi to running an army railway yard. The battalion of combat engineers that is attached to a division in the line has, as I have said before, only two missions: to see that drinkable water is available to every unit in the division and to solve problems involved in helping the movement of our troops or hindering the movement of the enemy.

Places where drinkable water is available are called water-points. You "put them in" when you arrive in an area and "take them out" when you leave. The process of putting in a water-point begins with a highly inaccurate map the intelligence staff has worked up. This shows where water is supposed to be—the streams, the ponds, the wells, which, in Africa, may be dry some seasons, overflowing in others. Map in hand, you make a water reconnaissance—drive out to check

46

the countryside against the map. With you, you take the little man with the gadgets. The gadgets are test tubes and chemicals that fit into a weatherproof box. They are to analyze the water you come on. On the judgment and skill of the enlisted man who carries this kit the division's safety from colic or cholera depends.

The putting in of our first water-point was like this:

In the distance, on the horizon line, there was a jiggle which might be trees. Yes, the map showed several wells somewhere around there. Trucks were coming and going along the road, and there was wire in the gutter, leading forward. Last night we had exchanged a few words with some officers we happened to pass in another peep, and didn't one of them say something about the 18th being out this way, ten or fifteen miles beyond the fork there? If the wells weren't dry, or the water not too far down for the pumps to suck it up, we could put in a point there and save the 18th the twenty-nine miles they now had to haul their water from back in town.

The 18th was one of the three infantry regiments of the First Division. In the line it was not called a regiment but a combat team, for it was composed of the 18th Infantry plus a battalion of field artillery and mobile anti-tank guns and some other units which made it a well-rounded fighting force. Building on its three infantry regiments, our division had three combat teams in the field and we had to look out for all three of them. They might be, and sometimes were, spread over fifty miles. Sometimes orders came down to us through our own engineer battalion headquarters for some service one of the combat teams wanted, or, as with water-points, which were routine, we simply kept track roughly of which troops were in what areas and tried to get our water-points in before they were asked for.

By the time we came to the trees on the horizon, we had overtaken the combat team and along the road we passed the little yellow markers which indicated the headquarters of its various units. To the right and left of us men were digging foxholes and making breastworks. The desert rose in a gentle slope to a flat crest and then fell away again. Back of the crest, they were siting the anti-tank guns.

The anti-tank guns were big 75's on ponderous truck chassis, almost as heavily armored as the tanks themselves. Their crews were digging emplacements on the side of the hill and after they had smoothed the surface out, the trucks drove in so that their rifles lay where they could just shoot across the crest of the hill.

There were no pup tents up yet. The gun positions and the foxholes came first. You could tell there was a command post on the crest of the hill because there was a group of officers there, with a command car and a motorcycle nearby. Two of the officers were looking forward across the plain with glasses. We made a detour to ride by them.

The infantry colonel, who was one of the men with glasses, came over to us. We told him that maybe we could find him some water over by the trees. He said fine, and would we come back and talk mines with him. We said we would and went on—as casually as that.

There were several deserted Arab buildings near the trees. We found two wells, round stone wells with stone troughs next to them. The Arabs hauled the water up to the troughs for their animals. But the water was no good to us because looking into the well we could see that it was thirty-five or forty feet from the surface. Pumps will not suck water that far. But a few miles away we saw some more trees, and there was another well there that was not on the map and the water was only a few feet below the ground.

We wandered about while the water tester unpacked his kit. He sat by the edge of the well, dipping up water, pouring it into test tubes and adding chemicals which turned first one color and then another. Then he said simply, "It's O.K.," and began packing his kit away. The first part of the job was done.

Now we took him back to our own command post, past the troops that were digging in, past the thickening train of trucks that were bringing up more men and more supplies.

From the command post we sent the man with the testing kit off to find the rest of his squad with their equipment. He would lead them back to the well he had tested. There they would presently arrive with a truck full of pumps and filters and the material with which to set up a big canvas storage tank, ten or fifteen feet across and four feet deep.

In half an hour the water-point squad would have a big suction hose down the well and the water would be coming up into their filters. With chemicals and the filters, they would purify the water according to the advice of the little man who had tested it. The water might come out of the well a sick and smelly green; when it came out of the filters it would still be greenish, but it would smell of chlorine instead of slime and no one would be sick from drinking it. It would go into the brown canvas reservoir and before the reservoir was more than a few inches deep the water trucks would begin coming in from the nearby units. No messengers would have to be sent out; within a few hours every unit within twenty miles would know where the engineers had put in a new water-point and the trucks would come to it like homing pigeons. All we had to do was to put the point in.

Since there were usually trees near where there was water we did not even have to worry about camouflaging the installation. We simply tucked it away in the shade and tried to keep too many visiting trucks from crowding in to make a thick black dot on the plate of the enemy observation plane's aerial camera.

We were always putting in or taking out water-points. Partly because the outfits were always moving in or out of this place or that, and partly because our pumps were so thirsty that they often sucked a well or a brackish pond dry. Then a man from the water detail would hitch hike into the company command post and stand around near where the C.O. was until he caught his eye. And the lieutenant would know, simply from the shake of the man's head, that the water had been used up where he'd come from.

The man would go off and sit down and rest until we

found him another point. Three or four hours later, riding by the command post on some other errand, we would remember we had left him there. Meanwhile, we would have found one or two other likely spots. So we would pick him up and take him out or send him on in another vehicle if we had one. All very casual, but things got done.

By the second day in Gafsa, company A had wire—that is, the signal company had a telephone line in from battalion headquarters and we had a field telephone in a leather case hung up on a tree. We also had the company's command car back. It had been lent to the general to ride around in the first morning.

The company's command car, like all command cars on the battlefield, was fitted with a big black radio sending set in the back seat. Its aerial was a willowy sixteen-foot rod which stuck out from behind the rear seat and banged against every tree we went under. The command car's crew consists of the driver, who is in charge, and a radio operator. The radio operator thought the driver ran under trees for the sole purpose of annoying him by banging the aerial against the branches. When six feet of aerial fell off and we lost it, the wireless operator would not speak to the driver for twenty-four hours. Finally, when their feud began to get on the lieutenant's nerves, he told them both to get out of the car and there he explained patiently that it was the fault of neither.

Besides the radio, the back of the command car was always equipped with assorted impedimenta and mud. There were rifles, rations, extra clothing and the lemons we stole or swapped for cigarettes—two handfuls of lemons for one Chesterfield.

The command car, in case you are confused by army nomenclature, is the overgrown, foreshortened, high-hung touring car that you have often seen around army camps but which you have never ridden in because civilians are usually transported in staff cars. The command car has a canvas top and when it is up, old-fashioned side-curtains take the place of doors and windows. It is a big powerful brute and can wade through heavy mud or light underbrush. Its seats are wide and deep and leather covered and on the back of the front seat—where there is a rack for an automobile rug in your sedan—there is a hinged shelf which can be lifted up to make a desk for whoever rides in the rear seat. On this shelf maps can be studied and orders written. The orders go out over the radio.

Doughboys don't go joyriding in command cars. When the Luftwaffe has any extra ammunition, its pilots like to pick off command cars, to get the officers they know live in them. For that reason, while doughboys do not ride in command cars, neither do generals. Generals ride in peeps. But company and field officers have to work a lot of the time in command cars, so they and their drivers are always alerted. At the first sight of a black speck in the sky the car is off the road and stopped and everyone who was in it is fifty yards away from it, crouched down with a pistol or a rifle in his hands.

When it rained we kept the top up. The minute the rain stopped the top went down and everyone's head went up, scanning the skies and the horizon. There is only a few seconds warning when a ground-strafing plane comes over. No enemy fired on us while I was in company A's command car, but one friendly fighter plane came over so low that it had to lift itself when it crossed the road above a 2½-ton truck. The strafing planes fly just above the ground so that they can only be seen a few hundred yards away. They will probably be gone before even the most alert gunner can fire a burst.

In their turn, strafing planes have only seconds to aim. They come across or down a column, opening their guns and dipping their noses just as they come in range. There is a splatter of lead and a whirl of dust. They have done their damage and they are off. Mostly, with the top up, we looked for dive bombers or for JU-88's—two-engine light bombers—

doing horizontal bombing from only two or three thousand feet up.

Whenever an enemy plane comes over, everyone shoots at it, purely for his own peace of mind. Not until you see the bombs fall out of the bomb rack do you flatten out and try to pull your head back into your body and then squeeze your helmet down over your body. That is, presuming there are no foxholes or other shelters, which there never are when you are caught riding on a desert in a command car.

Most of the time when engineer officers are riding around in command cars they are on some mission having to do with mines. Division engineers, as I said above, are concerned with water and the movement of troops. Mines are an impediment to motion. So to the combat engineer falls the job of detecting and removing the enemy's mines, as well as the assignment of laying "friendly" mines to impede the movement of the enemy.

In the last war, during which mines were not used so extensively, engineers had most to do with roads and bridges. When the infantry was held up by a river it was the engineers' job to put a pontoon bridge across it, working under fire if need be. There were few streams to be bridged in Africa—if there were many we would have had to double the number of our engineers in the line. Eighty per cent of the line engineer battalion's work in Africa was in mine fields.

Both mines and mine fields are simple devices. A mine is simply a charge of explosive buried in the ground with an igniter so devised and attached that any disturbance of the ground will set it off. There are a number of different kinds of mines but the ones that you read most about in the paper are those used to blow up either vehicles or men. The mines used to blow up vehicles are called anti-tank mines and the ones used to blow up men are called anti-personnel mines. The latter are more familiarly known as booby traps.

The anti-personnel mine, or booby trap, has two uses. It is sometimes used simply to kill unwary individuals who may come on it in a deserted house, say, or along a path. But its commonest application is as bodyguard to an anti-tank mine. It is attached to the anti-tank mine for the purpose of blowing up anyone who tries to disturb the latter.

The standard German anti-tank mine is known as the Teller mine. It is shaped like a very big, thick, black pie—eighteen inches across and several inches thick. It contains nine pounds of TNT. Over this ugly piece of pastry there is fixed a device known as the spider. The spider is well named. It is a frame of light metal which sits spider-like on top of the mine. When the mine is "alive," the spider is up and if you press on it, bang goes the mine. The pressure necessary to explode the mine can be adjusted. The usual adjustment is for two hundred and fifty pounds—so that a man could step safely on a mine but a vehicle following him would be blown to pieces. (To use nine pounds of TNT to kill one man would be an extravagance.)

The Teller anti-tank mine is usually buried about six inches underground. The German soldier who buries it is quite safe because even if he has screwed in the activator that sets the mine off—the activator is enclosed in a six-inch length of half-inch pipe—he is protected by an important little gadget. This is a brass pin about an inch long with a ring on the end. It is inserted in the igniter and a nut as well as a clamp holds it in place.

You can read the whole success of the German army in the safety pins of its Teller mines. They are gadgets which are to be thrown away. The cheapest cotter pin Ford ever made for his model T would do the job as well. Yet the Germans make these pins of brass and they are machined like watch parts. They are at once thoughtfully and skillfully made, with expense obviously no object. The cases in which the German engineers carry, not the mines themselves, but simply their spare parts—these cases are so beautifully made that they are prime prizes on a captured battlefield. Where the lid fits the body there is a heavy band of good springy rubber which countersinks into another strip to make the joint wholly waterproof. They are light and rugged.

When the German engineer has put his mine in the ground, he unscrews the nut from the end of the safety pin, unlatches the clamp and pulls the pin out. Then he fills in the hole over the mine and, if he has time, he tries to make the ground on top look as if there were no mine there. But even the most methodical German doesn't usually have time enough to do a good job of hiding the physical traces of a buried mine. For anti-tank mines are not laid singly, but in fields.

A mine field is simply an arrangement of mines, usually in a geometric pattern of carefully spaced rows, like plants in a very formal garden. A shallow mine field may be only half a dozen rows deep. There is still much debate about how close to each other mines should be laid. The accepted formula is one and one-half mines per yard of frontage. The mines in the second row will be staggered so that they line up between the mines in the front row. The idea is to have enough mines close enough together so that no vehicle can pick its way through the field without one of its wheels or treads running on at least one mine.

After the German has put in the Teller mine, but before he pulls the safety pin and covers the hole, he sets the booby trap—attaches the anti-personnel mine. One doesn't find booby traps on every anti-tank mine in the field. There are simply enough booby traps so that sooner or later, if precautions are not taken, the engineer who is "lifting" the anti-tank field will run on a booby trap and be blown to bits. After that other engineers may be presumed to be hesitant about proceeding—at least about proceeding as fast as they had been.

There is nothing new about the enemy's booby trap. The American army has known about and used such mines for a generation. The German booby trap is a flowerpot-like contraption about four or five inches across and six inches high. It contains two charges. The first charge, which goes off when the mine is disturbed, is of black powder. In itself, it is harmless. Its job is simply to throw the second charge into the air exactly as the kind of fireworks that we call a flower-pot throws colored balls into the air.

The lethal weapon that the anti-personnel mine throws into the air is a charge of TNT packed in a fistful of small steel shrapnel balls. It is set to explode four or five feet above the ground. The steel balls are likely to do serious damage to anyone within a number of yards, but booby traps are not always fatal. I have met two men who, on different occasions and in different theaters, had the misfortune to step on one. They showed me their scars but both are very much alive and quite well.

There are two standard types of igniters for mines, the push igniters and the pull igniter. As the names imply, one goes off when you push against it, the other one when you pull on it. Teller mines, of course, are usually exploded by push igniters. You might attach a pull igniter to a booby trap if you wanted it to be exploded by a man tripping over a wire hidden in a darkened doorway.

Newspaper reports—and the terrors of the imagination—to the contrary notwithstanding, mines are not particularly difficult either to detect or to remove. In the whole long inventory of the weapons of modern war, they are not only not the most difficult, but perhaps the easiest, against which to defend oneself. But they remain a powerful psychological weapon, as well as a nuisance. And amongst troops who are not familiar with them, or not alert to their possible presence, they may cause casualties.

The American mine detector—if you have looked at war pictures carefully you have seen them often—consists of a wooden disc stuck at an angle on the end of a wooden pole. The disc is eighteen inches across, the pole four or five feet long. It is an electrical machine and halfway up the pole is a control box with rheostat handles and a dial. You tune it as you would a radio set. The user carries the batteries which activate the detector, and straps the microphone which is con-

nected to it to his shoulder. When it is adjusted, this microphone emits a low, steady humming note. The man then
holds the detector so that its wooden disc is a few inches
above the ground and parallel with it. Then he walks forward.

When the wooden disc of the mine detector approaches
any metal object in the ground, the magnetic field that it
emits is disturbed and the note of the microphone changes—
rises sharply. When the wooden disc is right over the metal
object, the note is high and strong. The man who is using
the mine detector doesn't push his machine in a straight line;
he walks in a straight line but he swings his detector back
and forth in front of him, as if he were sweeping with a
broom held at arm's length. Thus he is able to cover a band
three or four feet wide. When he comes upon a mine he
doesn't stop to do anything about it. He simply indicates it
to the man following him, who marks the place. After these
two have passed ahead, other men come and remove the
mines that they have located.

How the American engineers remove German Teller mines
must wait for telling until after the war. The method is simple and foolproof and the battalion I served with, which
has probably removed more enemy mines than any other
engineer battalion at the front, has not had a single casualty
in the process. The division had had mine casualties but they
were almost always the result of mines off the beaten path or
of mines that had been overlooked in the course of a rapid
advance.

In rapid advances, our own mines were as dangerous as the
enemy's. In some sections of Africa the same ground had
been fought over several times and there were areas where
several German and several American mine fields had been
sown. When we came into one of them no one could be quite
sure that even our carefully checked and rechecked mine
maps had located every single one. If there was time, we re-
swept the area.

Mine fields in themselves are neither intended nor expected

to stop an advance. Their use falls under the head of delay-
ing tactics. They serve a military purpose not unlike that of
barbed wire—through which enemy troops must stop and
cut, dynamite, or trample a path before they can go farther.
The mine field's effectiveness, like the effectiveness of barbed
wire, is principally dependent on the effectiveness of "the
covering fire," the fire from the defender's guns which are
sited across the field. When the mine field is not under fire
there is no trick at all to going through it.

Usually, in the fast-moving campaign in Tunisia, neither
side had time to prepare its fields as the book would have
them. I know of no instance where an American advance
was seriously delayed by German mine fields, and the Eighth
Army followed Rommel from the Mareth Line to the hills
near Tunis at a full gallop.

These are important facts to remember, because of the
psychological element in mine warfare. As one officer at the
front put it to me: "You can give an infantry company three
hours to take a pill box in a hell of a tough spot, surrounded
by wire, and they'll go in and take it ahead of schedule, even
though it costs twenty-five per cent casualties to do it. But
if just before they take off you tell them that somewhere in
the enemy's position there is a single booby trap—well, they'll
all turn pale and their knees will begin to knock. You'll find
'em fooling around with that position for a couple of days."
My informant was indulging in dramatic overstatement, but
with green troops there was some truth in what he said.

The wholly effective medicine for mines is experience and
education. The officers of the engineer battalion I was with
did wonders by lending the infantry their mine detectors and
teaching them how to use them. Nothing seemed to give an
infantry column more confidence than a man with a mine
detector swinging out in front like a bagpiper, even though
its commanders knew that the engineers had already swept
the road twice the day before.

✦

Putting in "friendly" mine fields kept us as busy as taking out the enemy's. When he had left Gafsa, the enemy had dropped back fifteen or twenty miles. No patrols appeared to raid us when we went out beyond the forward positions to put in our mines but being out there made the blood run faster. First, there were the conferences at the forward command post. From where was the enemy expected to come? Where were our machine guns? Where were our batteries going in? Then we would pick out the positions on the map, and look out across the plain and try to see where who and what was. At that time, the orders were simply to defend Gafsa, to see that the enemy was "kept out of artillery range." We wanted no shells falling on the troops and vehicles that were clustered in the groves.

There were no natural defensive positions to the east of Gafsa. Beyond Gafsa in two directions, there stretched two great sweeps of flat land separated by a high, rocky bone of mountain. The mountain was so high and its sides were so steep that it divided the two plains into two battle theaters. The mountain itself was good for nothing except maybe an observation post—when a detail had time enough to climb it. Across one plain crawled the rutted track which was the road to Maknassy; a macadam road with two branches which led, respectively, to Sfax and to Gabes, went out the other plain, almost due east. Our job had been to make these roads impassable.

8

TO defend these plains beyond Gafsa, the first week we were there, the division could do no more than move a combat team out to the center of each. The men dug into the hard sand as best they could. Beyond the farthest machine-gun posts we chose sites each day for as many mines as we could lay that night. At night, the working parties would at least be free from observation from the air.

While we worked, the infantrymen and the artillerymen worked too, bringing up ammunition and rations. The Signal Corps men got the wire down between the command posts and the observations posts and ran wire back to division headquarters. The ambulances came up and the medical officers checked sites for their clearing stations. The men cleaned their guns first and then dug their foxholes. Finally, here and there, pup tents went up. The men who had been sleeping in the open were now under cover again.

Company A's men moved in before the rain stopped the first evening. All that first day we had been inspecting the chaos the rain and mud had wrought. Where we thought we could be helpful, we sent one of the bulldozers up to pull vehicles out of the mud.

No one who has not seen it can believe the immobility of a mobile column when the mud is more than axle-deep. It doesn't matter that the main roads are hard. Motorized columns can use a road only to move from one place to another. They cannot halt on a road for even a few hours. Whenever they stop their vehicles must take off to either side, disperse. When the ground is wet they barely grind their way out, and when they try to start again, their wheels begin to sing and spin and down they go.

Not one or two or three of the vehicles stick; they all stick. And the men get out and try to lift them and throw rain-coats and tarpaulins under the wheels but these only disappear into the mud. Then the vehicles hitch themselves to one another, with the cables from their winches, but by now they are dug in to above the floorboards. There is nothing for it but to wait. The only comfort is that the enemy must wait too. While it is really stormy his planes will be grounded as well. The war is called on account of rain.

While it was still raining, as I said, we found billets for company A under cover. First we drove around the out-skirts of Gafsa, getting out to inspect each building that looked habitable. We looked at the hinges of the doors for wires that might lead to booby traps. Then we inspected the floors to see if they had been disturbed, and the shutters on the windows before we opened them.

The company commanders of other outfits were also out hunting for a place to dry their men. The few buildings there were rapidly filling up. The law of squatters' rights was in effect. A building or a group of buildings belonged to the man who saw it first—and left a sentry to guard his rights while he went back to bring up his outfit.

Finally, after an hour's hunt, we came to a pleasant little sidestreet with a row of stuccoed houses, each with its own flower garden between it and the sidewalk. The windows of the first houses we came to were smashed in and the doors hung empty and the gardens were mostly trampled weeds. We chose one and began to explore.

It had been a photographer's house. There were only two rooms in it, but the floor in one was piled high with photo-graphic paraphernalia and stacks of pictures of Italian belles in their wedding dresses and boys dressed up in evening clothes or in uniforms. There were some pictures of Arabs.

While we were looking at them, a very old little lady in black came in and began talking Italian at us. Piecing together the expressions and gestures, we could follow her. She lived next door. This had been her brother's house. Her brother was now in prison in Algiers—the French had arrested him. She wanted us to be sure she was very happy we had come and we were quite welcome to the house and she would help us clean it out. And how long, please, before the war would be over? She was very old—at least ninety.

The photographer's house was all right and we could use three houses across the street from which all the furniture had been taken. They would be all right after the filth and the water had been swept from the floor. The water had come in through the broken windows and made desolate pools on the tiled floor.

We sent back to the grove for the company and just before it turned dark our column rolled up the street, the big 2½-ton trucks and the kitchen truck, followed by the peeps. The first sergeant came over to confer with us. His platoon sergeants went into the empty buildings at once to stake their respective claims. The kitchen truck rolled past and circled a row of empty buildings to rest under a big tree behind them. We had had supper several hours before, standing in the rain in the other grove, handing up our mess kits and getting them filled in the truck, and then eating quickly before the rainwater diluted and cooled the stew. But now at dusk the rain was stopping and soon we would have a roof over our heads. The C.O. said to the first sergeant, "Just get them under cover tonight and tomorrow we'll sort things out."

From somewhere in the bottom of one of the trucks came the officers' cots. The men carried them in and stood the bundles in the corners. While they were unpacking the rest of the stuff, we set them up in the midst of the trash. From the trash we fished odd pieces of cloth and cardboard and stuffed the windows so that the light would not shine out. Then we lit two candles and unrolled our bedding rolls on the cots.

We were well inside the limits of the village and there were troops all around us. The sergeant thought one sentry was all we needed and the skipper agreed. He told the sergeant to let the men sleep until seven. Everyone was in except one second lieutenant and his platoon. They would be out all night scratching in mines. The rest of us took off our outer, or wettest, clothing and our shoes, and climbed in between damp blankets. We were asleep without conversation that first night. Other nights we would sit in the candlelight and talk and talk and then go on talking after we were in bed, like kids in a boarding school with no monitor around to hush us up.

The skipper of company A, Lieutenant Cobb—the young man who'd been getting his hair cut the day I met him—had been an aircraft designer. He wasn't quite sure how he had gotten to where he was. He'd had a reserve commission from his ROTC in college, and when the war started there was a lot of talk and correspondence about his getting commissioned in the Air Corps. He was also an essential employee in an essential industry. But one day in the middle of the correspondence, orders had come for him to report to an engineers' camp. He said he was tired of waiting so he had gone. He had a wife and a baby. He showed me their pictures and the other lieutenants kidded him about showing them to me. Then one second lieutenant said, "To hell with it, I want to show him my girl's picture," and presently we all showed each other all the snapshots we had with us and talked about the different parts of the country we came from.

Cobb was about twenty-six or twenty-seven. His four second lieutenants were younger than he. Only one other had been any kind of an engineer in civil life. Cobb and he were very interested in mines and how they worked and had all kinds of ideas for their improvement.

The five of them had become so close that they were like brothers. Cobb was, of course, the eldest brother. But the others seemed to have arranged themselves until each, according to his temperament and how bright he was, had a

fixed place at the family table. The youngster who was fig-
uratively at the foot of the table was the baby of the family.
The others seemed fond of him but were inclined to leave
him out of conversations. He would venture remarks from
time to time, but nobody would let him finish saying what
he started.

By the second day out, the family had adopted me. The
colonel had said something about my reporting back to battalion, but the brothers would have none of it. "Battalion
doesn't care, forget it," they said. "You'll see a lot more with
us. Besides we need company."

To hear the brothers speak of battalion headquarters and
what went on there, you would think it was in Algiers and
its officers remote and protected from the realities of war.
The officers of A company respected the officers of the other
three companies of engineers. These were equals. But the
officers at battalion were old fogies and could not possibly
understand what life was really like.

The brothers were very proud of their men and told fabu-
lous lies about them. The company clerk who moved in with
us the next day was, they said, the foremost scholar in the
army. He had been, they assured me, the dramatic critic on
a big New York paper. He had read everything in the world
and there wasn't any question he couldn't answer. Besides,
he was a writer and would write the history of the company
one day and all of them would be famous. So-and-so—in
hushed voices—was a killer; the finest soldier in the outfit, but
you had to watch him to be sure he was killing enemies. The
killer was an old army man who had been first sergeant until
the brothers concluded that he did not understand soldiers
who had been in the army only eighteen months. How good
company A's cook was, was a military secret which I must
guard with my life. If the battalion ever found out what he
could make Spam taste like, he would be transferred and
then the war would not be worth going on with.

The brothers had written a song about the First Engineer
Battalion with twenty or thirty stanzas to it. It was a narra-

tive and traced the history of the battalion from training camp to training camp, from maneuver to maneuver in America, and then across by convoy to England. It mourned over the Scottish weather and grew excited over the impending departure for no one knew where until the southbound convoy was three days at sea. It told of the landing on the Mediterranean coast and the trip up to the front—wherever the First Battalion goes, there goes rain—and of the first battle of Medjez-el-Bab and of holding the Pass at Kasserine and of the move into Feriana. While I was with them, they wrote the first verse about Gafsa. They were always going to find pencil and paper and write this ballad down for me, but there never was time.

It's hard to say why there never was time because we spent so much just talking. While we were waiting for details to come back between trips out into the field, in the early morning after mess, and at night when there was shelter in which we could light candles, we sat around and told stories. I had a lot of stories to trade because I had been traveling from one end of Africa to the other and I had stories of landings in Morocco and Algeria.

When new troops came to town in Africa and new friendships budded, all conversations began with an exchange of confidences over where each party landed. The men who landed together at any given beach were fraternity brothers who had shared a common initiation. Conversations between the members of one fraternity and another always included reminiscences and accounts of the respective baptisms of adventure.

Experts will agree that landing on a hostile shore at night is one of the most difficult of all military maneuvers. Even before the opposition is met there are baffling problems to solve. First and foremost, there is the problem of navigation —of finding one's way to the place on the map that Intelligence has recommended for the landing. Celestial navigation at its best, even granting the luck of a starry night, is accurate only to within three to five miles. A landing beach may be a half mile of sand set in the middle of twenty miles of rocky, surf-torn shore. The radio beams which have long guided mariners to and from harbors in foggy weather are useless to an invasion force because they make the enemy a present of your intentions. Some very effective secret devices were used to solve the navigation problem in Africa. But some of them were then still new and experimental and they did not always work. As often as not, the confidences that were exchanged about the November landings in Africa were confidences about how far which assault waves landed from which beaches—and how they found their way back and what happened then.

There is, for instance, the story of the commanding officer who set out from some miles at sea to catch up to the assault waves that had gone ahead. In his Command and Control boat—a fifty-foot cutter—he did his own navigating and when he edged cautiously to an unfamiliar shoreline he found it strangely silent and deserted an hour before dawn. Sensing that he had lost his way, and fearing to lose it again, he waited until the first light to identify landmarks. It had been an unhappy hour of waiting and when he found—he had no doubt whatever now that he could check his map with what he saw with his own eyes—that he was at a spot twelve miles from where he should be, he began to sweat in earnest. What greater humiliation could there be for a commanding officer, setting out to lead his troops into battle, than to arrive after the battle is all over!

The chagrined C.O. went up the coast with his cutter's motor wide open and when he got to the right beach—yes, this was it, there was the steeple in the village and there were the road and railroad crossing so plainly marked on his map —there, instead of his bringing up the rear of his column, he saw the lead boats of his assault waves only now approaching the shore from the other direction. They had been lost, too.

I asked him if he had admitted to his officers that when he

met them he too had just arrived. Sheepishly, he answered, "Well, I didn't admit it for several days."

The most brilliant landing maneuver on either coast was the arrival of a battalion of Rangers on D day on the split second of H hour at a beach that was no longer than a single New York city block set in a solid cliff of mountains that extended for some miles either way. The plan had been one of great daring. The battalion's mission was to silence a battery known to be on top of one of these peaks beyond the beach, commanding the town on the far side of the mountain, where a larger landing was scheduled for several hours later. The battalion was to land at this out-of-the-way beachlet, climb the mountain and deliver its surprise attack from the rear. It did all these things and was completely successful.

This success had been so obviously dependent upon the precision of its navigation that I was curious to know which of several secret devices it had used. My efforts to find out were not only in line of duty—for I was there to study landing techniques—but were also spurred by a great curiosity about how this spectacular feat was accomplished. Yet it was odd that official reports and informal conversations proved to be alike only in their vagueness on this one specific point. I was in the vicinity for several days and it became an obsession with me to find out what had happened there that dark November morning at 4 A.M.

The answer, as answers sometimes do, came in the most casual of conversations—this one with a lieutenant who had been part of the main attack on the far side of the mountains from the Rangers. Out on the point that hid one attack from the other, but visible from both beaches, there was a lighthouse. The lieutenant, remarking on the whimsicalities of war, let slip, "You know, I'll never understand how the French came to leave that lighthouse lit. The rest of the shore was blacked out."

I do not say that the British landing barge crews who set the Rangers ashore on that pinpoint of a beach could not have done it in the dark—they made other landfalls that were almost if not quite as miraculous—but I do think it was cozy of them to forget to mention the fact that a French lighthouse keeper had led the way. And it was kind of cute of the American officers and men to join with them in their innocent conspiracy.

Whether the Frenchman who left the light on was a friendly fifth columnist or whether he simply forgot to put out the light when the whole coastline had been alerted, I never was able to discover.

Decorations were another favorite topic of conversation—how (and whether) they had been earned.

My favorite story about decorations concerned a young lieutenant who landed near the port of X. There was a battery of French 75's firing on the beach and almost every shell that it lobbed over came down to wreck a landing craft, to destroy a dump of food or ammunition or otherwise to disturb the assault force. The lieutenant captured this battery singlehanded and marched its officers and men back into our lines at the point of his tommy gun.

Now it is not often in war that a battery of field artillery is captured intact and very rare indeed that this is done singlehanded. So the commanding general was impressed. He and his staff considered a decoration automatic and it was only as a matter of form—and to satisfy his personal curiosity—that the general sent for the lieutenant to get his story first-hand.

The lieutenant had an honest, open face. He was shy and respectful. The general was very cordial. He sat the lieutenant down, lit the young man's cigarette and said, "Now—tell me *all* about it." The lieutenant fiddled with his collar, looked ill at ease, and began:

"Well, sir, I know I should not have been there but somehow I got separated from the men and I thought the best thing I could do was to find out where all that firing was coming from. So I walked towards the noise and when I got on top of that hill—you know, sir, the one beyond the railroad—I saw that it was a battery position. The battery was firing, and when I got close enough I saw that the soldiers were French." Here the lieutenant hesitated and began to squirm in his chair.

"Well," said the general, fascinated, "what happened then? Were you scared?"

The lieutenant said, "No, sir, but I was mighty worried. All I could think of, were your instructions about how to handle the French. You remember, sir, that your orders were not to fire on a French soldier unless we were absolutely sure that he was unfriendly. I thought, how can I tell for sure? And then I remembered that we had a countersign so that if they were friendly French they would know the reply."

"You thought," said the general, very slowly, "that you had better challenge the battery that was firing, in order to be sure it was unfriendly?"

"Yes, sir," said the lieutenant, brightly, "and that is what I did. I cupped my hands and hollered and when they did not have the right answer I knew I should have to make them prisoners."

"What did you holler at them?" asked the general.

The lieutenant looked perplexed. "Why, you remember the countersign for that night, sir. You must, sir. It was 'Hi Ho Silver'—and they should have answered 'Away.' So I cupped my hands and hollered 'Hi Ho Silver' at them."

"And then?" said the general.

"Oh, then they put their hands up right away—they surrendered, sir."

This story has been the subject of a great many mess table debates in Africa. The lieutenant did not get his decoration and many thoughtful officers are disturbed by this. They think the lieutenant should have been decorated for his coolness in walking up to the battery position at all—and for that quality which is even rarer than courage in battle: the quality of complete and literal candor.

Africa in the months after the invasion was full of stories about the kind and quality of the French resistance. Some of the stories had grim and tragic endings. There were many places where the American army met the ultimate test and paid in blood for its principles.

At one spot an infantry regiment was held for two days outside the gates of a village which could have been destroyed by an hour's shelling but for the commanding officer's respect for the civilians who were hiding helplessly in their cellars but could not escape so long as the French troops continued to obey Vichy's orders and resist our advance. The men who died before this town—and there were many of them—died for American honor and died well.

There is also the story of the capture of one Foreign Legion post. The humor in it is a soldier's grim humor, for men died there too—both French and American. They died honorably, but if the first stone well had not been full when the attack began no one need have died at all. It was the first well's being full that caused all the shooting.

The American officer who told me the story of the Foreign Legion post had led the attack. The post was four or five miles in from the shore and it was marked on his map as one of the landing party's early objectives. He was a lieutenant and he took the first company of men he could gather on the beach and set off.

They met no opposition on the march and the lieutenant recognized the objective he sought by its white-walled barracks-like buildings, visible from a long way off. He had no way of knowing whether the Legionnaires would resist so he immediately surrounded the place, stationing his men carefully. Taking cautious cover, he worked his way to within hailing distance and shouted at the buildings to surrender. He shouted several times and saw heads appear from behind buildings and then duck. Finally, to show he meant business, he fired his pistol into the air. Immediately a machine gun began to chatter and bullets kicked in the dirt near his feet. The fight was on.

It did not last long—just long enough to cause a score of casualties. The American lieutenant accepted the surrender of the post from an unhappy French lieutenant of the Foreign Legion and was surprised to find, when he inventoried the post's defenses, that the several hundred men there had had only a handful of rifles and two machine guns with which to defend themselves.

It was not until a week later that the American found out why the Foreign Legion post had been so lightly armed when it was attacked—or learned the sad fact that if he had dallied another twenty minutes it would not have been armed at all. Three days after the skirmish, had come the armistice. A few days later, in the interest of the entente cordial, he dined at the mess of the officer who had been his prisoner but was now his ally. It was an occasion that called for wine and wine was forthcoming. After the wine had warmed him, the lieutenant of the Foreign Legion, explaining his reaction to the whole episode, spoke volubly.

"You cannot understand," he said, "the dilemma I was in that morning. I myself had known that you might come. I felt that you were the enemy of my enemies, for I detest the Boche. But if you came, how should I conduct myself?" The American lieutenant said he could see that the French lieutenant had been in a spot. The latter continued.

"It was more difficult than you can imagine because while I knew at once that I wished to surrender, it is the Foreign Legion's unshakable tradition never to surrender. But then I thought, 'I have overlooked something. There are circumstances under which even the commander of a post of the Foreign Legion may surrender it—and that is if he is without arms to defend himself.'

"When I recalled this fact," the French lieutenant continued, "I was no longer in doubt. If there were no arms on the post when you arrived, there would be no reason why

I should fight you, so I began at once to dispose of the arms. There are two wells, monsieur, on the post. To dispose of arms, one must dispose of them so that they cannot be picked up again and fired. When I heard from our scouts that you were advancing from the beach towards the post I immediately—before it should be too late—began collecting our arms and throwing them into the nearest well.

"The really unfortunate part of the whole episode, my good friend," the lieutenant sighed, "is that the first well was already filled with arms at the precise moment that you fired your first shot. To have gone on to the other well now was obviously unthinkable. It was too late. Now that we were under fire, there was no way to uphold the tradition of the Foreign Legion but by fighting with what weapons we had left. I could not regret it more, my dear good friend."

These were the kind of stories we told each other at the front, telling them carefully and making them last and trying to get all the laughs there were in them. I had the best stories because I had been more places and had heard more different story-tellers: the officers of company A told their stories better because each man threw in a line or remembered something the others had forgotten and they told all their stories to each other often just to pass the time. A good story is a precious commodity in the theater of war and everyone will help the story tellers to put one over.

Most of the stories we told were true, or had been true the first time they were told.

I add this last story only because it shows the tricks an apprehensive imagination can play on you. If I had been spirited away from the field before the peep got back, I could have told about the crash of a mortally wounded airman with great verve—because I would have been sure I had seen it with my own eyes.

It was one afternoon at a bomber station and I was sitting with the medical officer, who was a major, and a second lieutenant who was what I think is called in the Air Force, the field officer—that is he was in charge of traffic on the field for that particular day.

One mission of eighteen medium bombers had gone up to the front an hour and a half before and they were due back any minute—which was why the ambulances were lining up beyond the medical officer and why the field officer was there with his peep. A half mile beyond the ambulances there were two wrecking trucks and a fire engine. No one knew what kind of luck the bombers had had or whether they had been attacked or had run into heavy fire from the ground, but everyone was ready to do what he could if trouble rode home with the bombers.

The lieutenant noticed the fighter plane first. It was a twin-tailed P-38, which wasn't right to begin with because there were no P-38 stations within a hundred miles of us. And then it wasn't behaving properly either—it was flying around and around the field and it was flying jerkily. Its wings tipped uncertainly when it banked and it lost and gained elevation irrationally. We stopped talking, the major and the field officer and I, and watched. While we watched, the P-38 made one last wobbly circle and suddenly began dropping fast towards the field.

"He's coming in crosswind," yelled the lieutenant, and started for the peep.

"His undercarriage must have been shot away," shouted the doctor and the wheels of the ambulance had begun to turn before he caught up with it.

The P-38 came down, dead crosswind, with its landing gear retracted and hit the ground at a hundred miles an hour, smack in the middle of the runway where the bombers were due to land any minute. Its flat bottom tore across the ground. Neither the field nor the runways were macadamed and the huge cloud of dust that exploded around the crashing plane was like the burst of a mighty shell. The fire engine was off, the wrecker was off, the driver of a second ambulance couldn't contain himself and he was after the pack, too. As for me, I had been too appalled by the swift approach of obvious tragedy to move. I could have ridden out in either the ambulance or the peep if I had been quick enough but I just stood and watched and in my imagination I saw the bullet holes in the P-38 and the blood on its pilot, bravely bringing his crippled craft into the nearest airport. I even looked into the sky to see if there were any pursuing enemy aircraft.

And then out of the dust and confusion in the center of the field there came the field officer's peep. But when I ran up to learn the worst and the peep stopped at my hail, the field officer was not there, there was only a boy who could not have been more than eighteen and didn't look within four years of that. He was a second lieutenant and he wore a very natty uniform—pink trousers tucked into highly polished Brazilian boots. And he spoke in the drawl of the deep, deep south.

He said, "Ah wonder effen you can tell me where thah's a 'phone round here. Ah think Ah ought to call somebody up about this. Ah don't think they are going to like it because Ah got lost an' then forgot to put mah landing gear down."

How his own squadron commander liked it I do not know. I am soft-hearted and felt very sorry for the young man who had lost his way in the air and come in in a panic and wrecked his $40,000 plane in a crosswind landing with his wheels up. I know how the bomber field's medical officer felt because he drew up alongside us a minute later. He said, "Young man, it is my studied opinion that you should be shot."

I got on well with the five officers who had lived so long together that they were like brothers, and I had fun with them. The middle one I will always think kindly of. Somehow ages came into the conversation and I admitted to being forty-two. "My God," said the middle brother, "I thought you were about Cobb's age," and, speculatively, "prematurely bald, I guess I thought." None of them ever asked me any personal questions. Mostly what they wanted from me was news of the America I had left many months after they had gone out. They had read no American newspapers since December and were very sober when they heard about point rationing and that gas was really hard to get.

Like everyone else in the American army in the theater of war, they lived only to get home. To get home—"to get back to tell my lies"—that was their war aim. Next to getting home, again like every American soldier in every theater of war, they wanted to be some other place than where they were, any other place. When they were in England they wanted to get to Africa. As soon as they were in Africa they wanted to see Iceland, or, "Gee, I'd kinda like to know what it's like in the Pacific." If they could not get to the Pacific, Gabes, sixty miles behind the enemy lines, would be better than here. To get some other place, to get home—these are the principal aims of the American soldier on the battlefront —until someone close to him has been killed or wounded. Then he adds to these emotions the sullen and persistent and sometimes savage desire for revenge.

To get on with winning—so as to get home—can become a desire so strong that men will and do risk their lives to satisfy it. When we stopped to chat with officers or men around Gafsa, sometime or other the grumbling would start, "God damn, what are we sitting on our cans for, why don't we go in and get them and get this thing over with?" These were not new troops, but troops of the best-seasoned American division in the African theater, men who had been fighting almost daily since they had landed west of Algiers. I think they had been out of the lines only once and then only for a few days. And yet they were always impatient: "Let's get on with it."

Otherwise—the danger of death and destruction to one side—it was a pleasant life they lived. To these men it had long since become a life in which finding an empty house for shelter was a real luxury—something to lick the chops over. This is not said in sympathy but to show that, everything in life being relative, these men were now accustomed to lives in which simple comforts gave them great satisfaction. Food at the front was plentiful and good. If the diet was monotonous—the C rations plus a not very wide variety of canned meats and vegetables—the cooks at the front, without exception, were abler at their trade than the cooks in camps at home.

The C ration is a set of six small cans, the contents of each of which is different. Two of the cans provide one man with breakfast, two are the staples of mid-day dinner and two are for supper. The best-liked C ration can is the one with baked beans and hunks of meat and vegetables. One of the cans contains candy and crackers.

C rations were for when we were on the move. When the kitchen truck was on hand, a typical day's menu in the line would start with either scrambled eggs or wheatcakes for breakfast. The eggs would always be scrambled because they come in cans, powdered. One day the cook told Cobb that he had been "attempting an omelette, sir, but the experiment has not yet been a success." Along with the main breakfast dish, there would be canned apricots or prunes and hardtack or crackers and coffee with, maybe, condensed milk. For dinner, you would get fried Spam, canned succotash and—if there had been luck with the weather, and the time to bake it—bread. There would be plenty of butter but it had so much preservative in it that it tasted waxy. For supper there would be thin frankfurters split in two and fried, or cut up like Tootsie Rolls and mixed with some vegetables in a stew.

If the cook is given any kind of a break he can make this fare taste as good as any wholesome meal eaten outdoors after a hard day's physical work in the open. The monotony is the worst feature. The mess sergeant's only chance to vary it is to pick up vegetables or fruit from the countryside. When an army moves in, however, supplies don't usually last very long. The lemons that were two handfuls for a cigarette the first day in Gafsa could not be purchased for love or money a week later.

Armies are like locusts—they devour the country through which they pass. The Americans were thoughtful locusts and a strenuous attempt was made to leave more food with the natives than we ate up. C ration cans were plentiful and popular locally. We usually gave away several dozen a day to anyone who happened to wander by company headquarters—an Arab on a camel, French or Italian kids, any village official.

After my first few days with company A I felt like a veteran. My helmet ceased feeling strange on my head, and I felt as if there had never been a time when I hadn't worn side arms. I reacted to the three whistle blasts that warned of enemy aircraft in sight as quickly and calmly as I once reacted to a change of traffic lights on a New York City street. I felt at home and curiously at peace, with useful and interesting work to do and pleasant and easy companionship. I noticed it with others who came up to the front: men adjust quickly to life in the field. There is an easy democracy in a bivouac in a forward area. Junior officers and men often eat and sleep together, everyone knows everyone else's jokes and eccentricities and all are dependent, each one upon the others.

I had been with company A about a week when I was ordered to report to battalion headquarters for another assignment. Reporting there in the morning—of D day, as it turned out—I was at once a little sad to be leaving the brothers, and relaxed into boredom as the day wore on and I waited for the colonel to come back and tell me what next.

And then the orders for the attack had come at five o'clock in the afternoon. And now it was after seven and it would happen any minute. For two hours, two years, two lifetimes I had sat thinking as preparations for battle went on around me. Suddenly I felt again, as I had felt in the plane in Algeria, a sharp sense of my own inadequacy. The grenades in my lap, the pistol at my side and the rifle that I was dusting with a rag did not make me a soldier. I was not a soldier and only a battle *might* make me one. Well, now it was here. It was suddenly very quiet in the orderly room and in the square outside. Everything was ready now, as ready as it would ever be. I thought of a sentence in a letter an Assistant Secretary of War had once written me about the army of the United States. "I hope," he said, "that you find the army well prepared for the ultimate test it is soon to undergo." I had no idea whether either the army or the one-four-millionth of it that was I were well prepared. All I knew was that a small part of the ultimate test of which the Secretary spoke was about to begin.

It was nearly 7 o'clock. I thought of the Germans and Italians. I thought, and it made me laugh thinking it: Ready or not, pal, here we come.

PART II

An Army Is Quite a Thing

1

IT is not simply that I like to talk about the army. I want to tell you about the army because I want you to know; there is that much of the teacher in me still. I think you ought at least to know what an army is. It is not simply rhetoric to declare that this is your army. Yet, I found out two things about you after I got back from Africa. One is that the gaps in your knowledge of the army are big, obvious, and unnecessary; and, two, that you really want to know. Everywhere you ply soldiers with questions which sometimes they answer partially and sometimes they are too tired, or too interested in something else, or too inarticulate, to answer at all.

So this part of this book is time out on the edge of the battlefield to talk about what it is that fights battles. An army is a complicated thing—it's no corner grocery store. By all means, if what I have written seems too dull or too obvious to you, skip it. Go on to the next part, where the march into battle begins again.

Here is my idea of a *minimum* of the knowledge that you as a layman should have, in order to understand the organization that you have created for the purpose of fighting your battles. You may know all these things; if you do not, you should mistrust your critical judgment. You should know that you cannot tell how well or how badly a game is played until you have mastered at least the rules.

There are many misconceptions, I have found, about the life of the soldier in the field. The American soldier emerges, in the photomontage of journalism, as a kind of individualistic adventurer living in something called a foxhole, too shy or inarticulate to tell you how he feels or what he has experienced, but with a rare sense of humor and an ever ready wisecrack. It is surprising, considering how many words have been written by and about soldiers, that even the most elementary facts about their lives still make a blurred and confused picture in the public's mind.

They speak, of course, a language of their own—a soldier's language of initials, abbreviations, technical terms—and they refer to individuals as well as organizations by numbers and still more initials. A few of these terms, like G.I. (for Government Issue, meaning standardized or orthodox) and K.P. (for kitchen police or unpleasant), have found their way into common usage. The people at home are learning. But few of those who buy the war bonds which pay the soldier's salary can yet give clear answers to such elementary questions as what's the difference between a C.P., a C.O. and an O.P. Nor can they tell you what a corps is or what a staff means. The amateur military expert at the dinner table who can talk with authority on envelopment movements could not draw an accurate picture of even such a simple device as an anti-tank mine.

The strategy and politics of this war have been well reported and the papers are full of dramatic and moving eyewitness accounts of heroic action; but most soldiers, I think, will agree that the American public, watching the war in which it is so vitally concerned, is still like a young girl watching her second football game. The purpose of the long runs are clear to her, but she knows little of the play in the line that made them possible and nothing of the intricate training that led up to the scene that so excites her. There must be a reason for this, for the American public no doubt tries hard to understand what is happening to its sons and brothers and husbands on whose skill its future as a free people depends.

I think the reason is that the time when a soldier learns what an army is and how and why, is during the months he is in training. There he learns faster than he ever thought he could learn anything, not only because of the pace of training, but because the life is so different from what he has left. Everything is new and vivid to him and he is wholly preoccupied with learning, and must learn a great deal in order to survive at all. But during this time, the soldier is out of touch with his old world. He is too tired to write. When he tries to talk he finds that, anxious as his listeners are to know, there is too much to explain, too many terms to translate. And what the hell, he didn't come home on leave to talk about the army. He already lives in a world apart and he can now only really exchange his thoughts with others in that world, others who know the terms and relationships—and the values as well as the initials.

By the time he has really become a soldier, the ex-civilian has accepted all this and when he writes, he writes of the humor of the life, as Private Hargrove did, or tells his stories of extraordinary adventures to journalists, as in *They Were Expendable*. Most of the best correspondents know what an army is and how it works. But they would no more think of writing its ABC's than a political analyst in Washington would think of writing about ward politics in terms of individual voters and politicians and how the candidate really got elected. The correspondent is an instructor in a postgraduate course, not a teacher in a grammar school. Yet, in thinking of war and battle, unless you really know a little of the vocabulary and the grammar, you cannot be sure that you have the right answer or, in fact, that you are anywhere near the truth.

Take so simple a proposition as the effect on the tide of war of "Who has the best tank?" You think there should be no difficulty in answering such a question? If the enemy has a tank that is bigger, stronger, faster, better armored and with a more deadly gun, then would you say the enemy will win all the tank battles? But consider the facts: in Tunisia the Germans had such a tank in their famous 60-ton Mark

VI. And yet, instead of winning all the tank battles, they actually won none. They won some engagements, but no battles.

With limited knowledge to evaluate it, the oversimplification of the question would lead the average man to a wholly erroneous answer. Many factors conspire to rob what seems a conclusive advantage of its power to be decisive—principally, as in the case of the Mark VI tank, what few laymen really understand: that it is not the weapon in the arsenal that counts; it is the number on the field in working condition, in the hands of experts. The Germans had the biggest tanks, but they simply did not have many of them.

The ultimate objective of an army is to impose its collective will on the enemy. But its first mission is simply to exist. Its first problem is to feed and clothe and shelter itself, and to be able to move itself from one place to another. Most people think of an army as expending its energy in fighting the enemy. Actually, most of an army's energy goes into keeping itself alive and in being; and in getting itself to where a very small portion of its numbers can fight an equally small portion of the enemy's total army.

As soon as we won in Tunisia, we had no place for our army to fight the Reichswehr. But even when Rommel's armies were still terrible, a surprisingly small portion of the Allied "armed forces" in Africa was engaged in fighting it. And of those who are entitled to battle stars on their ribbons, only a small fraction were killing in the literal sense. And even the killers spent most of their time—I would guess an average of twenty-two hours out of twenty-four—in housekeeping for themselves, and in moving from one place to another.

Yet the whole effect of the army is as integrated as the shaft and the head and the point of the tip of a spear.

A human being is such a frail thing that he cannot live more than a few days without both food and sleep. Nature is still his real enemy even though he takes his eternal struggle with her for granted. So the army as a whole must survive against nature before it can harm a single enemy by even so much as a scratch on the finger. The business of surviving and moving itself from one place to another is ninety per cent of the army's business, and unless it does this well it is not an army.

The army solves its problems of surviving by two dull words: organization and standardization—and an enormous personal effort and submergence of the individual will to the collective welfare.

The organization of the army starts with its smallest unit which, in the infantry, is the squad. Squads, at various times and for various purposes, have been different sizes, but the standard squad—the G.I. squad—is twelve men. From there on up you can learn army organization like the multiplication table: three squads make a platoon, three platoons make a company, three companies make a battalion, three battalions make a regiment, three regiments make a division (three regiments—three sides to a triangle—hence the term "triangular division"), two or more divisions make a corps, two or more corps make an army. A nation may have as many armies as it has the men to create. And all the armies together, plus some other elements, make up *the* army.

The individual soldier at the base of this pyramid, in theory, has one sole responsibility: to be obedient to the authority of the army. This authority is vested in the commissioned officers of the army; what authority the noncommissioned officers have, the sergeants, the corporals, the privates-first-class, is simply delegated to them temporarily.

For each unit in the army, from the company up, there is an officer of an appropriate rank, who is absolutely and completely and finally responsible for everything that goes on in his unit. He must see that it is properly fed, clothed, and sheltered, and even its state of mind is his responsibility. These unit responsibilities are linked together in what is called the chain of command. It leads from the platoon lieutenant up through the commanding officer of the company to the commanding officer of the battalion, etc. The commanding officer is always referred to as the C.O., until the rank of general is reached, and then he may be called the C.G., the commanding general.

The theoretical rigidity of this chain of command is not always understood by the public—the completeness with which the C.O. is responsible, as long as he is C.O., until he is "relieved of his command." A colonel cannot explain away the defeat of his regiment by putting the blame on, say, one of his captains. He, and he alone, is responsible for all the units under his command. If one of his captains fails, the blame is still his. He is guilty of "an error in judgment" in putting the wrong captain in command of the company that failed.

Captains and lieutenants are known as company officers; majors, lieutenant colonels, and colonels are field officers. From the lowest field officer commanding—the major—upward in the chain of command, each commanding officer may have the service of a staff. Staff officers are advisers to commanding officers. They are without authority in the chain of command.

All the advisory—the staff—functions of the army are divided into four parts: part 1 is Administration and Personnel, part 2 is Intelligence, part 3 is Training and Operations, part 4 is Supply. Many a feature story and magazine article has listed these functions by number but they slip easily from the layman's memory. Nevertheless, they are the warp and woof of the American army's organization.

The numbers one to four have one of two letters in front of them—S or G. S1, S2, S3, and S4 refer to the staff functions of units smaller than a division. G1, G2, G3, and G4 refer to the staff functions of divisions, corps, and armies. Until you are thinking of the army in terms of its G's you are not thinking accurate military thoughts.

Next: any one of the four G's (or S's) is two things: it is at one and the same time a function and a man, who is responsible for the function. It is a function, a man, and, in staffs of any size, a section of assistants, officers and men, and their files and office paraphernalia and the place on the map where they work. Thus, G1 is a man whose function is to advise the commanding officer on matters of administration and personnel. It is also the function of keeping the records of individuals, shifting their assignments, promoting them, transferring them, etc. And it is the group of men, the sub-organization, the place, where these things are done.

So the commanding officer of any unit larger than a company is served by four men who may or may not have assistants to help them. He is served by G1 as above, by G2 in matters relating to military intelligence, by G3 on how his unit should be trained and how it can best operate to achieve its mission in the field, and by G4 on its supply problems. Each staff function will have a different mission when in garrison and when in field. G3's duality of mission is the clearest: G3 is the schoolmaster at home, the maker of battle plans on the field.

The efficiency of any unit will depend on its staff—on whether G1 picked the right men to recommend for promotion, on whether G2 is really intelligent about the enemy's strength and movements, on how sound G3's training doctrines were and how effective and imaginative are the battle plans it recommends; if the supply system breaks down, G4 has been giving bad advice.

But remember, before you go on, that the G's are advisers only. They are not links in the chain of command and they administer only their own sections, if they have any. You may hear a soldier criticize a battle with some such speech as this: "The plan was all right but the intelligence was not good. We ran into a battery that wasn't on the map." He was praising the work of G3 and damning G2, for the commanding officer, while he is solely responsible, had obviously to rely on the knowledge and wisdom of his staff in writing his orders.

That's enough about army organization for a moment. I feel like telling a story, and this is one of my favorites about the landing in North Africa.

Honor is not a fashionable word amongst American doughboys, and in their shyness they underrate it as a military weapon. Honor has been known to stop an armored column dead in its tracks; not honor in general but the personal honor of one man in particular. There were no reporters present and his name, age, and address were not recorded. But it happened, truly and exactly as I record it, one night in Morocco.

The armored column was American. It was a full division strong and had landed the day before. Its mission was to proceed inland from the coast to parry a blow that was expected from up Marrakesh way. Its encounter with honor took place about one o'clock in the morning, just as it wound into the foothills of the Atlas Mountains.

Now an armored division in column formation is a fiercesome thing. Closed up for battle, it stretches fifteen miles of solid steel and fire power. It can blow a good-sized town off the map in thirty minutes. Yet, honor pinned it to the ground, held it choking and roaring with its motors idling for three precious hours in an enemy country in the first phase of an historic invasion. Had there been more resistance in Marrakesh when it got there the next day, it might have lost the battle. Credit honor, with an assist to sentiment.

The general in command of the armored column was a very active sort of man, bluff, aggressive, short and sturdy of stature and red of face. He is a brilliant soldier and his men adore him. He rides into battle with them in a jeep with the top down, accompanied only by his aide who drives the jeep if he is not so impatient that he takes over the wheel himself.

At the moment it began, the general had thus jounced through the inky black, in and out of the gutter, to the rear of his column, just to be sure that all was well there. The rear of a fifteen-mile column moves characteristically in long waits and short rushes to catch up. Therefore, it was some time before the general realized that there was something unnatural about this particular wait. In such close proximity to the enemy there was, of course, radio silence. So it was some time before he diagnosed the wait not as minor traffic trouble but as something more important. Fifteen miles, he suddenly thought, my God, maybe with all this noise of running motors I can't hear the firing! Maybe we have made contact! Maybe we are being ambushed.

The general's aide has been under fire many times and he did not get his job by being a timid man, but he recalls no terror like the terror of that ride up to the front end of the column with his suddenly alerted commanding general. As the long steel column had halted, it had crushed up upon itself on a narrow road so that there were places where not even a jeep could wedge between a stalled M-1 tank and a steep embankment. In such emergencies, the general would climb the bank and proceed on through the woods, "bouncing," the aide swears, "from tree to tree."

Thus came Sheridan to the battle fifteen miles away, ten miles away, five miles away—but as he approached the battle-field there was not more noise to greet him, but less. For here the drivers of the mighty tanks and the fiercesome tank destroyers, resigning themselves to the wait which was now stretching into its third hour, had shut off their motors and climbed out to gossip in whispers by the roadside. And against this new silence, after the throbbing of the motors and the clanking of the treads, there was still no sound of gunfire to account for the halted column.

The general and his aide covered the last few miles. The front end of the column was stuck into a densely wooded mountain pass. They swung around the last sharp turn and this is what they saw: One 23-ton M-1 tank and, just beyond, a semicircle of American officers and men, their helmets silhouetted in the bright light of a lantern shining from just ahead of them. The general leapt from his jeep and strode through the group. The officers and men were silent, for they had long since exhausted words. Beyond them and in the center of the road there stood—as he told me the story, the general enumerated the items, counting on his fingers:

One rock, almost round, about three feet in diameter.

One lantern, kerosene, sitting on rock.

One soldier, French, aged 75 with snow-white beard, and across his faded tunic, row upon row of ribbons from each of which hung a medal.

One rifle, 1870 government issue, in hands of said poilu, its butt resting on ground.

"And what," asked the general, halting before this tableau, "what the hell is this?"

The old soldier with the beard squared his shoulders and answered firmly but respectfully, "Monsieur, c'est un road block *symbolique*."

"And why, may I ask," said the general, whose French was still adequate, for he had learned it well in the last war, "why is it there?"

"It is there," said the old man proudly, "because *I* am guarding it. I represent the honor of the French army. It is not possible to permit the invasion of French soil without resistance. So you see, monsieur, I resist.

"It is true," the old man continued, "I can only resist symbolically. But I resist"—and letting his eye rove sternly over the semicircle of American officers—"and I resist not unsuccessfully, monsieur. There is no argument by which these men can persuade me not to resist."

The general had learned more than the language in France. Slowly and thoughtfully he walked around the stone to the old man and with affection and respect he put his arm around his shoulder. "Old one," he said, "I am glad I have seen what I have seen. But this matter is not as difficult as you imagine. It is now clear to the whole world that you have done your duty. It is very late and I can assure you— for I am the commanding general of this column—that you may now go back to your bed and sleep in peace."

Tears of gratitude for such understanding came into the old man's eyes. He grasped the general's hand. "No, no, monsieur, now I cannot go. You have made it impossible."

"But . . . but why?" asked the commanding general.

"Because," said the old man, drawing himself up again, "I have inconvenienced an army that was once the ally of France. I must now stay and help you to remove the symbolic road block."

"It would not," said the general with just a slight catch in his voice, "be fair to these men of mine, who are so young and so anxious to serve. *They* will remove the road block, Papa; they will remove it *for* you."

And so it was that the road block *symbolique* was at last pushed to one side and the motors roared and the mighty steel juggernaut rolled on, passing a spot that should forever be a shrine to the honor of France—and to the fine sensitivities of the American soldier in foreign parts.

And now to get back to the army as an organization:

Think of the army as a pyramid of commanding officers, each wholly responsible for the men and officers under his command, and each surrounded by a group of at least four advisers, one for each of the basic advisory functions.

In addition, the C.O.'s who command units as large as divisions will have additional advisers. They, too, will be staff officers, on the C.O.'s special staff. (G1, 2, 3 and 4 are called his "general staff.") The divisional commanding officer may have a score of special staff officers. The chaplain and the head of his military police will be on his special staff, so will the engineer officer, the signal officer, the senior medical officer, the special adviser on artillery, etc. He may hear any or all before he commits his final decisions to orders.

Each commanding officer is as responsible *to* the next higher commanding officer as he is responsible *for* his men— the only important thing to note here is that as the chain of command ascends to higher altitudes, each successive commanding officer will have greater latitude in the execution of orders that are passed to him. The commanding general in the theater may simply order the commanding general of one of his corps to take such and such a city, leaving the battle plan wholly to Corps. Corps in turn will specify that one of its divisions is to proceed to such and such a place and deliver a flank attack, but will leave the details of the attack to the commanding general of the division. The importance of understanding this fact in analyzing the news becomes immediately apparent.

Toward the end of the Tunisian campaign there was much confusion in the press over the role of the American Second Corps. Military analysts in America did not know how much or little autonomy its commanding general had. Was he a bad or timid general, or had he been given insufficient troops, or were his supplies inadequate when he failed to cut off Rommel's retreat from the Mareth Line? Without specific knowledge of the relationship between the general commanding the Second Corps and his superiors in the chain of command, criticism or praise was pointless. General Alexander commanded Allied ground forces in the theater and General Eisenhower, in turn, commanded the theater which included these ground forces. It was only *after* the battle that General Eisenhower publicly revealed the limit that he had set on the Second Corps' mission: to guard the supplies which had been stored for the British Eighth Army's present use, and to contain the German army on the coastal plain while the Eighth Army delivered the main attack. Once this was clear, the campaign could, for the first time, be analyzed. The limitations and the strength of the American forces were to be judged against the limited objectives that were set for them; the success or failure of individual divisions or of the corps as a whole was then to be measured not by what the people at home dreamed or hoped they might be able to do, but by their effectiveness in carrying out the orders given them.

It is not enough to appraise the achievements of an army with no more knowledge than who its commanders were and what limits were placed on their authority. Put Napoleon in any American general's place, there would still be only so much he could do with his troops the day after he arrived at headquarters and shook hands with the unit commanders he inherited. In fact, the first thing which would make or break him would be his judgment on what his troops were capable of. If he gave them a plan that was beyond their capacity he would lose the battle no matter how brilliant the plan. And the first important factor in the capacity of his troops would be how much of their energy they were using up in simply existing at all, and next how much they had left over for mobility, and only finally, after they had made the effort of feeding and sheltering themselves and the added effort of transporting themselves to where the general ordered them, how much they had left over with which to fight.

Too much of the Tunisian campaign was reported in terms of individual heroism under fire. And too little in appraisal of our effectiveness simply as an army.

As a machine built to deliver men in the field properly armed and equipped to meet the enemy face to face, the army is not the present commanders at all, but several generations of planners, whose plans had to include the whole industrial economy of the nation. On the wisdom of forgotten men and forgotten officers in the War Department in the twenties and thirties the dependence of our army begins. Hitler's mad inspiration may have given the Reichswehr a quality it did not have before. But not Hitler or even Rommel made the Afrika Korps. What made the Afrika Korps was a little group of experts in the war office in Berlin in continuous existence through victory, defeat, revolution and counter-revolution. And these are the men who chose and standardized the equipment of the individual soldier.

The American soldier is first created by his uniform, his pack, and his rations. All three are amazingly efficient. To understand the importance of the planning, remember what was so quickly passed over above: that the army, not the individual soldier, is responsible for his welfare. He doesn't plan his uniform as a civilian chooses his clothes, nor does he raise or shop for his food. Every necessity of his life is planned for him years in advance. The fundamental of the plan is that his clothes, food, and shelter must keep him healthy and self-sufficient without the help of civilian facilities. The plan had to start with providing for the soldier's well-being alone on a desert with neither barracks nor canteen nor any place to get into when it rains.

Line troops—roughly: troops qualified to take their place in a firing line—are self-sufficient neither at home nor in the field. Huge military organizations serve them. These, too, must be understood.

First there is the monster store that is known as the Quartermaster Corps. The Quartermaster Corps is a gigantic department store with thousands and thousands of branches, and the component units of the army are its customers. The Quartermaster Corps designs and manufactures or buys these stores and the component units draw what they need, paying in signed requisitions instead of money. The Quartermaster Corps is the largest service organization in the army.

To another semi-autonomous organization is entrusted all communications within the army. This is the Signal Corps.

The Engineer Corps builds (and demolishes) for the army and is responsible for all transportation the army cannot do on its own feet or in its own trucks or by calling on the navy to transport it—and for many other things.

The Medical Department is a similar semi-autonomous body. So is the Ordnance Department, which manufactures, issues, and maintains the army's weapons and, as a kind of sideline, its other mechanical equipment.

These great service corps, each with its own field of responsibility, are joined together in what until a few months ago was called "The Service of Supplies." Recently, its name was changed to the "Army Service Forces."

The three-star general, General Brehon B. Somervell, whom newspaper readers are most familiar with as the general who represents the army in the running dispute over whether army officials or civilians should "control" the War Production Board, is the boss of all the service organizations. And since his mission includes the supplying of the whole army, his interest in how production for the army is planned and administered is natural and inevitable, however you feel about whether he or a civilian should have the most say in how the contracts are let.

In theory, a unit of ground forces could exist simply by drawing its supplies from the Quartermaster Corps, having the engineers build barracks for it and the Signal Corps install the telephones—without the ground force ever being more intimate with the service force than you are with Macy's and the telephone company. In practice, what happens is this:

Each major unit of the army has units from the service forces permanently assigned to it. It is as if, we might say, you are so big a customer that the A & P opened a special branch for you in a room in your house, and, to insure domestic tranquillity, made you the boss of the clerks who worked there. Thus, a division may have a company from the Signal Corps attached, and whole battalions of medicos and quartermasters—as well as a platoon from Ordnance and a battalion of engineers. The commanding officer of these detachments are on the special staff of the commanding general of the division. Then, when the commanding general wants something built, instead of writing to the Chief of Engineers in Washington, he simply orders the commanding officer of his engineer troops to do the job. And each day, as the army on the move progresses, its attached signal personnel will see to it that all its units are kept in communication with one another, whether by wire or by wireless or with semaphore flags or by carrier pigeon.

And thus, finally, line troops with their attached service elements together at last make a self-sustaining, independent community that can exist and care for itself without benefit of civilian facilities.

Sometimes it confuses even soldiers in my own branch to

learn that the combat engineers, who held the line as infantrymen at Kasserine Pass, came, not from ground force General McNair's troops, but from General Somervell's service organization. It is this way: the service troops—engineers, signal men, medical personnel, etc.—are trained by their respective service corps, but are subsequently attached to and become an organic part of the ground forces. Their function in the field is always one of some specialized service, but any of them (except the medical men, who are limited by international conventions) are at the disposal of the commanding officer in the field to be used as fighting troops.

Except in the direct emergency, the engineers are the only service troops likely to be used as infantrymen. Signal Corps men, for instance, are much too important as specialists, and usually too few. The engineers, however, are intensively trained as infantrymen because their most important function at the front is to keep the infantry moving, and this means that on an advance they must build roads and bridges *in front* of the infantry. In a retreat, they will be the last to leave, for it will be their mission to impede the enemy's passage by blowing up roads and bridges or by building obstacles. Trained as infantrymen, there has hardly ever been a campaign in which combat engineers were not called on at some time to take over some of the line. The Tunisian campaign was no exception; the engineer regiment that held the gap at Kasserine for thirty-six hours had a higher casualty list than any infantry regiment during the campaign.

My first and clearest impression of the difference between the division at home and the division in the field was an impression of the merging of all these different units into a single working community, with each branch completely, and obviously, and pretty happily dependent on every other.

PART III

*"Chittenden to Henry, Chittenden to Henry.
Bring Up the Mortars. Over"*

1

THE shoes I wore were Government Issue, of heavy leather, ankle high and with thick crepe rubber soles. They were the shoes I had kept for Saturday inspections during basic training. Every day or two I had shined them, carefully laced them up, tied a bowknot at the top and put them side by side under the foot of my bunk. But I had worn them for a month in Africa and they had got wet and dried on my feet and now they were broken in and comfortable. I had heavy wool socks under these shoes and wore canvas leggings on top.

I had not been out of long, heavy underdrawers and a heavy wool undershirt for ten days now, and I thought, "I can stand the night if it doesn't get too cold." If you keep wearing woolen underwear against your skin and are careful not to bathe, the oil from your body gives the wool life again and it is warmer and resists the dampness. I had read that in an intelligence pamphlet on how troops should be prepared for embarkation. Some of the first men who came to Africa came in cotton shorts and suffered dreadfully from the cold. Those of them who had been torpedoed had not come through as well as the men who had been wearing wool and were unwashed.

My dark green dress trousers were the only fancy things I had on. Over my undershirt I wore a light wool sweater and then a flannel shirt and finally a field jacket. I wore a necktie because General Patton fined officers who didn't wear neckties $10.

I had my helmet and my web belt with pistol, canteen, two extra clips of ammunition and a first aid package attached to it. I had cleaned my pistol the day before, after I had found dust in it. I had taken it out to shoot at an observation plane that was circling so low it looked as if you could hit it with a stone.

There wasn't much else I could do to get ready for the battle. After I filled my canteen with fresh water from the canvas water bag that hung outside the door, I got out the musette bag that held all my personal belongings and considered its contents. I stuffed two packages of cigarettes in a pants pocket. I came on some benzedrine tablets a medico had given me at Camp Edwards, and I stuck them in my watch pocket. I had two D rations, which are simply blocks of compressed and vitamin-filled chocolate about the size of a package of cigarettes. I stuck them in a hip pocket. I thought, when I felt my wallet there, that I had with me more papers than I would like to have found on me on a battlefield. I had copies of orders mentioning units and I had notes on mines and mine-removal techniques. I took my wallet out of my pocket, and surveyed its contents.

I thought, "This is the time to do a little thinking. We are going back of the enemy's lines. A little money would be a good thing to have along." I took all the French money and all the American money I had—about $20 in French money and nearly $200 in American—and my officer's identification card and made a wad of them and put them in the pocket with the chocolate.

I came across a snapshot of the Connecticut farmhouse where I once lived and which still belonged to me. The picture was taken in the summer and the trees were in full leaf. I thought, if I had no other link with home I would like to be able to look at that picture. So I took out the wad of money and put the snapshot of the house in Connecticut in with my identification card and put the wad back again.

I put the wallet itself in the bottom of the musette bag and I took out a pair of thin leather gloves. I passed up a fur-lined vest because if the walking were to be hard I didn't want to sweat. I rummaged around for a compass that I knew had disappeared a week before. I still couldn't find it. Finally, I took out an extra pair of socks, stuck those in the other hip pocket and strapped up the musette bag, which I would leave behind me. I was ready.

While I sat waiting and thinking, D company's two lieutenants kept coming and going. When I mistook one for the other—both were young and had round, brown smooth-shaven faces and were about the same height—he said that people were always confusing them, and grinned. Each time one of the lieutenants came through, he stopped in his search through the gear on the floor and fished something out and gave it to me.

First, I got a handful of rolls of candy drops. "Probably won't be able to smoke," said the lieutenant. Then, the other opened a box of C ration cans. He stuffed several into the top of his field jacket and told me to help myself. Two cans were supposed to make a meal. I hunted for the ones with meat and beans in them and took out four of them and put them aside for myself. When one of the lieutenants came in with a tommy gun and began working the mechanism and inspecting it, I asked him if the company had an extra M-1 rifle. It was obvious that the officers and men of the hell squads were arming themselves with whatever weapons they felt most secure with. I asked for an M-1, a Garand, because it was the only gun I really knew how to shoot. Once on the range, I had got high score for the company with a Garand.

The lieutenant thought a minute and said I could have Captain Henry's M-1. When I hesitated, he urged, "Go on, take it, he never uses it. Wait till you see what he carries— he always takes that damn wop auto-rifle."

After I had Captain Henry's M-1 in my hand, I got a web belt with each of its pockets filled with clips of ammunition for the M-1. And then one of the lieutenants opened another box and it was filled with yellow hand grenades. He picked up two and dropped them in my lap.

Thus, as I sat there and the time passed and it grew dusk outside, I acquired weapons and food and ammunition. As the pile on my lap grew, I remembered the stock answer to the trainee who complains about the weight of his pack. "Listen, son," it goes, "do you know how they send a man into a battle? They run him through two lines of soldiers and each one throws on a bandolier of ammunition. This goes on until the sergeant sees his knees buckling under the weight. Then the sergeant himself throws on a bushel of hand grenades and kicks him in the tail and says, 'Take off.' "

There was no way I could help in the preparation of D company for the battle, and I sat there because I thought that was where I'd be the least nuisance. Back in the training battalion, when I had been bucking to make good—trying hard, because the sergeants were inclined to be suspicious of editors turned soldiers—I would probably have made work for myself. By now, I was enough of a soldier to know that I would only be a nuisance if I tried to help; these men had been in action many times and each had allotted tasks he *had* to do, and other things he wanted to do before he went out, and no one needed any aid or comfort that I could give. Later, on the field, if I behaved myself, I would find ways to be useful without asking.

No one knows how he is going to behave in a battle until he has been in one. Anyone who says he knows is making big talk. If I had never fought in a battle before, I'd been around battlefields enough to know that. What I felt, waiting before El Guettar, were two fears—fear itself of that kind of panic that paralyzes, and fear that my muscles would not be strong enough to do what would be required of them.

I had had bombs fall around me before and I had been very frightened. I had now the comfort of knowing that fright is like a hangover or bad seasickness—that it feels awful but that in itself it is not fatal and it will pass. But when I had been bombed before, in London or in Kharkov or in Chung-king, I had been a spectator. Nothing had been asked of me but that I behave no worse than any other spectator. But now I did not know what I would be called upon to do. I only knew that it might be like being bombed only worse and that, during it, I would be called upon to act and—what was harder—to think.

Back in Algiers—it seemed years ago now—my commanding general had talked to me just before I left for the front. He was an old army officer and had commanded a regiment in the last war. He said to me: "You mustn't worry if you get frightened, you know. Nine soldiers out of ten will tell you how frightened they were the first time they got under fire. The tenth," he said, "is a damned liar."

I was afraid, waiting for El Guettar, that if my fright was like very bad seasickness then maybe there would be nothing that I could do about it. If I were paralyzed by fright I would be helpless. I was very much afraid of being afraid.

As to physical endurance, I knew that I was in good shape. I also knew that being "in good shape" might not be enough. A man who is over forty learns about age for the first time in his basic training. He learns that if a company of men of many ages keeps marching long enough—long after the men with bad feet or weak legs have dropped out and until the rest are marching to survival of the fittest—he may not be the first who cannot go any farther, or the second, or the third. But the men of heart who are in their twenties will still be shuffling down the road when the old timers in their thirties and forties begin to break up—as they break up in the prize-ring or even on the ball field.

I did not want to break down in my first battle with men I did not know, and not even a friend near me. I had made the last march in training, the climax march with 40 lbs. of equipment on your back that always ends the course. But for one reason or another it had only been twelve miles over the low rolling hills of Cape Cod. And yet I'd had blisters the last few miles of that march, and that was nine months ago now and most of the time since then I had been an office soldier.

The platoon lieutenants came and went. When I got up and stood in the doorway, I could see in the dusk that the vehicles in the square were all packed now. The scene was quieting down. The men were standing in little groups, not talking. They had their helmets on and their rifles slung over their shoulders, muzzles up. You could pick out the hell squad boys for they wore hunting knives. Many of them had extra bandoliers of ammunition crossed over one shoulder and hanging down around their waist. They wore field jackets and most of the field jackets bulged with gear that had been stuffed inside them. Only the drivers stood by the half-tracks for the gunners were coming with us by truck.

Now the kitchen truck, with a trailer behind it, came out of the alleyway behind the building. The kitchen trucks and the half-tracks fell into column formation and went off across the square to some rendezvous where they would wait until they heard from us again.

It was almost dark now. Just before the moon rose, two planes came over and circled slowly above the town. After a few moments of uncertainty, a battery of Bofors began shooting at them with their characteristic half-choked, half-hollow sound. I thought, "I wonder what they can see from those planes. I wonder if there is much traffic on the road yet. There shouldn't be; it is still early for an advance that is not to begin until nearly midnight and an attack that will not start until dawn." I thought that maybe the two planes saw the roads empty and that, if so, theirs would be the last report for the night. It made me feel good, thinking that.

It was after seven, and I fastened the belt with the extra ammunition around my waist so that it held in the bottom of the field jacket—the pistol belt hung down around my hips—and I stuffed the cans of C ration and the grenades in the top of my field jacket. Now I bulged like a very pregnant woman. If the belt stayed in place everything was all right and I could walk easily.

The end of the wait came quickly. Captain Henry came

running into the room where I sat with the two lieutenants, all three of us booted and spurred. He spoke rapidly: "Hurry it up. Let's take off. They want us out ahead of the column. In another half hour the roads will be full." He was picking equipment up from the floor, hanging it on him or stuffing it in his pockets. "Ingersoll and I will go in the command car and I'll show you the way. I want Curran on a motorcycle along with us. This will be the order: first the hell squads and then the half-track squads carrying the mortars." He talked on in short sentences as he got himself ready. "The Ranger battalion we are going to join is out almost to El Guettar. We are going to fall in with their column. There is supposed to be a German regimental strongpoint out there, or German and Italian. We are going around behind it. But first we have to find those mines."

Captain Henry went over the timetable again: 8:45 with the Rangers, from 8:45 to 11:45 take up the mine field. At 11:45 the march was to start. After that we would take orders from the colonel of the Rangers—Chittenden was his name.

"I want Sergeant Chervassy with me until we get organized." Chervassy wasn't the sergeant's name but it was something as hard to remember as that and later, several times when I had to find him, I would forget it. But when I made up some complicated name like that, the soldiers always understood and pointed him out for me or sent to get him.

I trotted out at Henry's heels and climbed into the back seat of the command car. It was almost full of bedding rolls and coats and other equipment that was going to be sent to the rear after the car had taken us up. A soldier came out of the shadows and climbed in with me. He was Sergeant Chervassy.

All the vehicles but ours had gone from the square and now the motors of our trucks were running. We left the darkness under the trees and crossed the square to the road. On his motorcycle, Curran twisted by us and went ahead. The trucks came after us. I looked back to see how many there were but I could not count them in the darkness. There were sixty or seventy men in our company.

Henry was nervous now and he kept giving the driver directions to go faster or slower. The sergeant alongside of me gave the driver directions, too, telling him to look out for this tree or for that bump. The driver was very responsive to both sets of directions but he could not please the sergeant who finally asked if he didn't want to let him, the sergeant, take over. The driver said no he didn't and cut into the gutter around a truck he was overtaking. After that the sergeant relaxed, but Captain Henry did not. The few vehicles we overtook were hard to push over to the side of the road and Captain Henry got up out of his seat and stood on the command car's narrow running board and bellowed into the noise of grinding gears and throbbing motors of the convoys.

The moon was coming up, and riding fast without lights you could see a little way ahead but not enough for comfort. When we were on the wrong side of the road, passing something, it was frightening. I thought, this is going to be like the old gag about the bomber pilot who made twenty-one trips over Berlin and then gets smashed up in a taxi accident in London. But still it felt fine to be moving fast after waiting so long.

Sergeant Chervassy and I bounced and banged against each other and we began to talk. He wanted to know what I knew about what we were going to do tonight. No one had told him. He had been busy all afternoon, getting the men ready, seeing that they had everything and then stowing the baggage away and this and that. He made no comments which would indicate his attitude toward the action. He simply wanted to know what there was to be known. He received my meager store of information and seemed content with it. He showed no curiosity about my presence.

After a mile or two, we passed the last of the trucks going our way and after that we went along up the valley at forty or fifty miles an hour. The road was hard macadam and straight as a ruler here. Now, in the moonlight, you could see mountains to one side and desert to the other. There were no signs of life whatever. It took us a little over half an hour to cover the twenty miles to where we were going. Of the last minutes of the drive, I remember nothing but the wind rushing by and the easy springiness of the ride which was so unlike the riding I had been doing on rutted dirt roads and across the desert. Time stood still and there was only the pleasurable sensation of moving rapidly and comfortably through the dark.

I did not see the sentry who stopped us and when I got out it was as if after a refreshing sleep. The moonlight was already bright and we were underneath a cone-shaped hill that stood apart from the mountains in the background. It rose abruptly, 400 or 500 feet high. Our trucks were closing in behind us and the men were climbing down out of them, slowly and carefully because they had so many things hung on them. After there were men on the ground, the men in the trucks passed equipment down to them, guns and parts of mortars and ammunition for mortars. The sentry was a gray figure with a slung rifle. He was standing on the edge of the road.

The captain told me to get the men off the road and to tell them to spread out and get themselves some sleep. He said they were to wait here until the men who were going up to the mine field got back. He said something I never heard about why he had to go and where, and said he would be back by 11:30. Then he got into the command car again and drove off, with Curran following on the motorcycle.

The second lieutenants were nowhere about and I seemed to have inherited the company. As soon as he saw me there, the sentry came up and said very politely, "Excuse me, sir, but I am not supposed to let you have these trucks up here."

I thought, "He doesn't know that the whole division is coming up." But I said to him, "Why not?"

"Sir," he said, "whenever there's more than one vehicle here it attracts fire. That battery over there"—gesturing into the darkness—"fires on this road whenever there's two vehicles stop here."

That I did not like. I went back and told the men to keep coming out of the trucks. Then I thought they would move a little faster if I told them why. I said, "There's a battery that fires on this road whenever there are trucks parked here." One or two of the men began swearing to themselves or each other. The rest made no comment other than to move more rapidly. I went down the line and talked to each driver and told him to get set to swing around as soon as his truck was empty. I wanted to send them all back together. But some of the trucks had more in them than others and I thought that if I could not get them all out of range I'd better get as many as I could. So I told the drivers of the empty ones to get going down the road and stop a mile or two beyond and wait there until the rest caught up to them.

When they had their gear, the men climbed down off the road. The road ran over a five- or six-foot embankment here. The ground below was very rocky and the men slipped and scraped over the rocks. Finally, first one sat down and then another and then all were only vague shadows sprawled out amongst the rocks and some were stretched out prone and looked as if they might already be asleep. These were good soldiers who did not fool around about resting but lay down and let their muscles relax and saved their energy whenever they had a moment. The non-coms stood on the road until it was clear and then they too climbed down, but sat at the foot of the embankment, leaning against it, so that they would be nearest the road when the order to move came. I found one of the lieutenants. He had been closing up the far end of the column to see that there were no stragglers. He said the other lieutenant had gone up to the mine field.

In the darkness and being busy with the trucks I hadn't even seen the mine field party go. My watch said it was only half-past eight. I knew that the lieutenant ahead had two working parties, one on each fork of the road. I thought maybe there should be two officers up there so I left the other lieutenant with the resting troops and I walked up.

I walked a mile, maybe two, maybe three. I only remember that as soon as I had left the shadow of the conelike hill, the lieutenant standing on the road disappeared into distance and darkness. Looking back I could see no one. The moon suddenly became very bright and my shadow alongside me was sharp and black and I could hear my own footsteps. Suddenly I felt infinitely alone. I knew I couldn't lose my way for there was only one road, and somewhere on it ahead of me were the working parties. Just beyond the working parties were the enemy lines and the battery that fired on the road wherever there were two or more vehicles there. I was in what used to be called no man's land.

I said to myself, "What the hell are you doing here? This is crazy. Who told you this was the way to win a war, walking out to the enemy lines alone in the moonlight?"

I also said to myself, "Look, you decided to walk up here before you were scared and you must have had a reason then. So keep right on walking."

I had a long talk with myself along these lines. The only thing that felt comfortable was my helmet. Everything that had made my helmet uncomfortable before made it comfortable now. It felt big and heavy and looking out from under it was like looking out from under something safe. I kept peering out ahead of me along the road and to either side out over the desert. Everywhere there were boulders. There were big boulders and little boulders and they made shadows. I kept on walking and I kept on walking.

The first human sounds I heard were the sounds of another man walking. The shape of his helmet came out of the dim gray light. It was like my own. As we came closer, a matter-of-fact voice said:

"They are right up ahead. The road forks here, sir. If you look hard you can see them. There's one party up there to the right and another one out there to the left." And then, conversationally, "One of our patrols got a motor sergeant today. He was an Eye-tie. There's an O.P. right up on top of that point there and he had been taking stuff up to it. He seemed kind of glad we picked him up."

I said, "You are a Ranger sentry, aren't you?"

And he said, "Yes, sir, what's going on here tonight, anyway?"

He turned and we walked slowly up the road together toward the working parties. I said, "The division is taking off from here about sunrise."

He stopped and stopped me and, looking earnestly up into my face from a few inches off, said, "What's going to happen to the patrols, sir, I mean our patrols? They are out there now, two of them. If the division is taking off there will be artillery. There will be a barrage. Our patrols will catch it."

I said, "Not until after it's light, anyway. Maybe there won't be any barrage."

He shook his head and said, "They won't be back until daylight. That would be tough luck if they got hit by the barrage, wouldn't it, sir?"

I said I knew there wouldn't be any shooting until after it was light. I left the Ranger outpost still shaking his head.

He was right about where the working parties were. By looking carefully I could see dim forms ahead of me in two directions. Listening, I could hear the scraping of tools in the dirt. I took the left road at the fork. I remembered from the map that this was the road parallel to which we were going to attack. Half a mile from here it entered the mouth of a steep-sided pass. At the far end of this pass there was an Arab village called Bou Hamran. Beyond Bou Hamran the valley widened and the hills dropped down and rolled gently into the plain beyond. Across the plain, where this road led, was the coastal city of Sfax.

The road off to the right, I recalled, went through a different kind of pass, with mountains on one side and a salt lake on the other. Then it, too, reached the coastal plain. It fell away to the south and came out at the sea by Gabes.

When I came to the working party along the Sfax road,

they were almost done. I found the lieutenant standing in the middle of the road. He recognized me and said in a whisper, "Hello, quiet, isn't it?"

There were ten or twelve men with him, mostly on their hands and knees off to one side of the road. From the road you could see, in the shadows, the pie-plate pattern of the excavations from which they had already lifted the mines—rows of dark circles, evenly spaced. They had piled the fat round mines near where the lieutenant stood. The American mines are not as big around but are thicker than the German.

One block of mines had been set in the road itself. There were other mines in both shoulders of the road and in the desert that stretched to either side of the road. The mine fields were laid that way so that a vehicle could not avoid the trap by running off the road.

The men on their hands and knees in the moonlight were working their way across the sand, stabbing into it with their bayonets. They drove their bayonets into the ground exactly as if, instead of looking for mines, they were cutting asparagus stalks. The men knew where these mines were because these were the same men who had laid them, that is, they knew *about* where each mine was and the sergeant had a diagram on a piece of paper which he could not light a match to look at. To find each mine the men had to remember not simply *about* where each mine was but *exactly* where it was, in relationship to some stone whose shape could be remembered. Since no one could remember to the last inch where each and every mine was, the men had to hunt them with their bayonets.

When a bayonet struck the metal of a mine, the man felt it in the handle. Then, very delicately, he could scrape away the dirt, lifting out handfuls of it and finally touching the metal and feeling the round shape of the mine and the metal cross-pieces of the spider. Then, still feeling in the darkness, carefully, delicately, he came to the place where the safety pin went in, and he cleaned out the hole and, taking a safety pin from his pocket, he put the pin in again and the mine was safe to lift. After that he would work his hands down around each side of the mine and pull it up out of the ground. Now working rapidly and surely, he unscrewed the igniter and the mine was quite harmless again.

The men worked almost noiselessly. The only sounds were the scraping of the knives going through the ground and the little whispered consultations.

The sergeant was in charge. The lieutenant was there only for emergencies. When the last mine was up, the sergeant came over to where the lieutenant and I were standing, and said, "Sixty-five down and sixty-five up, sir."

The lieutenant asked him if he were sure and he said, "Uh huh."

The lieutenant said, "Take your men back to opposite the Ranger post—you remember that little hill where we got out of the trucks—and tell them to take it easy there."

The lieutenant and I walked back to where the roads forked and went out the other road. All was not going well with the second party. The sergeant there was grunting irritably. "There's one missing," he said, "and we can't find it."

He said the mines were all out of the road and they were all out of the shoulders, "but there's one out there some place," pointing to the right, "and God damn if we can find it."

The men were spread out like caddies and golfers looking for a lost ball. You could see that some individualists had their own ideas about where to look and were off prodding away by themselves. Others were arguing with each other in whispers. Half a dozen were disgusted and had given up and were sitting disconsolately on the edge of the road.

I could make out the dial of my watch—it was almost eleven now. We did not have much more time to look, for in forty-five minutes we had to be back at the Ranger post. The lieutenant cross-questioned the sergeant. The sergeant was very convincing about his count. The lieutenant said, "All right, it's on this side of the road then. Line everybody up in a straight line here and we go right over the whole business."

This is a very strange sight, I thought, sixteen men inching their way across the desert in the moonlight, stabbing bayonets into the sand in front of them. I looked about. The prospect of finding the last mine was not hopeful. Where the field had been spread out wide of the road, the pattern had been purposely broken and from the shadows of the holes where the mines had been you could see that the field was simply a clump of mines here and a clump there. Moreover, the men had been spading so long that all in between the mine holes the hard sand was scratched and chipped up. You could see there was now no way to solve the problem either by maps or logic. The line of stabbing men passed and re-passed over the area where the lost mine was supposed to be, their bayonets hitting nothing but stones. It was twenty past eleven when the lieutenant asked me what I thought.

"I think we are licked," I said. "The road's clear and the shoulders are clear and the columns going up will be sticking to the road here. I think if we tell the sentry he can flag the first people to come up in the morning and they can post a guard to keep vehicles off the sand this side of the road."

"You can't hold up a whole division for one God damn mine," said the lieutenant reflectively. "O.K., the hell with it."

He motioned to the men and they picked up their rifles and put the bayonets back in their scabbards, and we sent them on down the road ahead of us. He and I followed, walking rapidly.

The Ranger was still at the crossroad and we told him about the missing mine. He said he would stop the first vehicle that was going up beyond him and tell them to leave someone there to warn vehicles that followed. The men ahead walked even more rapidly than we and within a few minutes their shadows had melted into nothing and they were gone.

Once more it was silent in the desert. The moon above the mountain rim was almost perfect, almost full. There was not a handful of cloud in the sky. There was neither man nor manmade war anywhere, only mountains, desert, moon and silence. It was in a peep that the war came riding up to us again.

We heard the peep before we saw it and it stopped alongside us with a scraping of tire on macadam. There were two officers in it and a driver, and although the peep had been doing all the running, they were breathless. The one who stuck his head out whispered hoarsely: "Have the engineers got the mines out yet?"

I was nearest him and I looked him over, speculating on how to put it. I said, "The engineers have got them all out—except one."

"Holy Jesus," he said, "what kind of talk is that? 'All but one!' We've got to put in an artillery O.P. up there."

I said, "It's up the right fork and it's off the road. You will see where the mines are out of the road and it's right opposite there, on the right. You won't get into any trouble."

The officer said "Holy Jesus" again and without waiting for directions the driver put the car in gear and they went whirring off into the darkness.

When we came back to the place on the road where two or more vehicles usually drew fire, the whole scene had changed. In the space of three hours, an army had moved in.

2

BY eleven-thirty of the night before the attack, two of the division's three combat teams had broken camp and moved up to the jumping-off point near the Rangers' outpost. Where it passed the outpost on the cone-shaped hill, the road mounted a rise in the ground and was lifted still higher on its embankment. You could stand on the road and look back towards Gafsa, with the vast plain dropping away just enough so that you could see over the tops of the vehicles that now covered it.

The straight road ran parallel with the mountain range, only a mile or two away from where the foothills became steep. Pressed between the road and the mountain, and sprawled out on the side of the road away from the mountain, were thousands upon thousands of gray shapes, big and little, each casting its black shadow in the moonlight. Off to the left of the road, an anti-tank battery had scratched itself into the uneven rock and sand. The black steel barrels of its guns reflected the moonlight in lines of silver. Behind them, the first shadows that the eye picked out were of big vehicles, big trucks, tanks, weapon carriers. Between and amongst these monsters you could pick out the smaller shadows of the little peeps.

The vehicles were all motionless but still the plains seemed alive. The surface of the desert was in motion. The motion was slow and without clear pattern. Then you realized that the motion was of men—of many, many men, all moving— moving away from the road and up towards the front edge of the line of vehicles. The men were moving, some in lines and some scattered, without formation.

Listening, you could hear two sounds. You could hear from far away the sound of motors running; way back they must be still moving up the road; and from all about, like the sighing of the sea, there was the scraping and shuffling of thousands of feet on sand and rock. Through the shuffling noise, came the clicking of stone on stone, fainter still than the shuffling. And, still fainter, came the light clack of metal on metal, as someone loaded a gun or slid a bolt in and out or banged some piece of metal equipment against another.

Other than these there were no sounds, no voices, no normal sounds of movement.

Thus was the attack mounted and waiting. Thus we came to it, the platoon lieutenant and I, walking back to our own lines from the space between the lines which had been protected by a mine field which we had now removed. All that we saw in the moonlight would attack with the dawn.

The batteries near the Rangers' outpost were sited to fire down the road by which we had come back to the line. The officers we passed in the peep had been going up to choose a point from which they might observe the fire of these batteries. Presently, wire would go up to them so that they could telephone back when the batteries began to shoot, to observe and correct the fire.

There were two batteries sited near the Ranger post. One, you could see, was set to fire down the road that led to Sfax; the other down the road that led to Gabes. Now that our own mine fields were no longer in front of the lines to slow down any enemy force that might come, these guns would have to take over that task. The division was about to attack, and these guns were braced against counterattack.

This much of the battle plan I knew: that what we saw there on the plain was the making of not one battle but of two. There were two combat teams there which, with the dawn, would advance along each fork of the road. The success of the attack on the Gabes road was completely dependent on the attack that was to take the left fork towards Sfax. So our attack—the one on the Sfax road—was to be given six hours' head start.

The reason for this dependence was clear on the map. The right fork of the road, that led to Gabes, stretched across open plain, bounded on one side by a salt lake and on the other by the clifflike mountain wall. If an attack had no cover there neither had the defense. The road that led to Sfax, on the other hand, entered a mountain pass so easy to defend that military experts would be pardoned the use of the word impregnable in describing it.

It was shaped like a cross section of a funnel. Across the mouth of the funnel were wide belts of enemy mines—they were marked on our map—and behind these mines were thick aprons of wire. The narrow road between had heavy stone road blocks at intervals and more mine fields between them. Up the irregular sides of the funnel, placed each one above and behind the other, were gun positions dug into the rock. Either side of the funnel could cover the other side, and both sides fired out across the wire and the mines. There were anti-tank rifles and heavy machine guns and light machine guns and, farther back in the valley, 88-mm. howitzers.

It presented a fantastic problem in frontal assault. Our artillery could only fire on the position in full view on the flat plains, while the fire of all the enemy's guns interlocked to rain death on anyone who approached the mouth of the funnel on foot.

Now not only was this funnel difficult of entrance, but its mouth pointed out across the road that led to the other battlefield. If the column attacking on the Gabes road ran the gauntlet and dashed by to by-pass this death trap, it would be at the mercy of an attack launched from the mouth of this funnel. The enemy could here come out on the flank of the other battle.

So the funnel that led to Sfax had to be first put out of action and then captured before it was safe to advance in the other direction.

Capturing the funnel, then, was to be our objective; our two missions were first to deny the enemy the use of the funnel, thus protecting the flank of the other battle, and, second, to take the funnel itself as a second avenue of exit from the mountains to the plains in Rommel's rear. The funnel would always be a secondary avenue because the road to Sfax was a dirt road and, as I presently was to find out, very vulnerable to bombing in the narrow neck of the funnel. The hard-surfaced road was the one that forked to the south towards Gabes, and in that direction there were no narrow bottlenecks.

"*Our* mission"—"we" were one of the three combat teams of the First Division. Our combat team—called the 26th—had the First Ranger Battalion attached to it. Company D of the First Engineer Battalion was in turn attached to the Ranger battalion. That means that "we" were some 2,500 infantry-men, plus a battalion of field artillery and other components of a combat team—a total of 5,000 men.

Our most useful artillery that day were 105-mm. guns. The American 105 is a cannon which shoots a shell about four inches in diameter and a couple of feet long. It can throw the shell seven to eight miles.

We also had some anti-tank howitzers. The howitzer is a cannon with a short nose. It is lighter and easier to handle than the 105-mm. but it cannot shoot as far. The anti-tank howitzers were mounted on trucks. The big 105's had to be towed to where they were to be fired.

The First Infantry Division is motorized infantry, which means that it is equipped with enough vehicles—trucks of various sizes, half-tracks, command cars and peeps—so that it can be moved from one place to another on wheels. Many of these vehicles are armored but it is not an armored division, the distinction being that when it goes into action it gets out of its vehicles and fights on foot.

Infantrymen now fight with a wide variety of weapons. Behind their peeps they tow 37-mm. anti-tank guns, minia-ture cannon. As the name implies, these are the tools with which they defend themselves from attack by tanks. On the offensive, however, the infantryman must rely on what he can carry. The artillery that supports him will fire over his head, to blast the enemy out of his way, but he himself must fight on foot with what he can carry. Infantrymen carry two sizes of mortars, several kinds of machine guns and automatic rifles, rocket launchers, hand grenades and an attachment so that they may shoot hand grenades from some rifles. They also carry rifles, both hand operated and semi-automatic, and some .45-caliber pistols, bayonets and a few knives.

The mortar is the infantry's own personal artillery. It has a short round barrel, untapered, like a three- or four-foot length of stovepipe. This barrel stands on the ground, locked into a metal plate about the size of a small table top. Its folding legs hold the front of the barrel so that it is cocked up at a sharp angle to its base plate. It stands almost vertical. The mortar is not loaded from the breech, like a rifle or a cannon. There is no breech. The bottom end of the barrel is closed. One loads and fires it at the same time, by dropping the shell down the muzzle. Dropped down the muzzle, the firing charge explodes when the shell hits the bottom of the tube and then, instantly, it comes back up out of the mortar with a great whir and an enormous bang.

The mortar shell then proceeds up into the air in a great lob, going very high and curving over and dropping an easy rifle shot from where it started. The shell looks like neither a cartridge nor a cannon shell but like a small aerial bomb. It has a rounded point on one end and on the tail there are four fins to steady it in the air. A mortar is aimed by setting a stake in the ground in the direction one wishes to shoot it, and lining up the barrel with the stake, then adjusting the elevation of the barrel with hand screws.

The mortar is a rough-and-ready instrument: its high lobbing shell is easily blown off its course by wind and you cannot knock a clay pipe out of a man's teeth with it. But its great virtue is that it is easily taken apart and a squad of men can carry the pieces and put them together at a place wholly inaccessible to artillery. The barrel makes a load for one man and the base a load for another. A third man carries miscellaneous accessories and the rest of the squad tote ammunition. The mortar is carefully contrived so that the heaviest piece of the biggest mortar weighs only about forty pounds, just about the weight that a rookie is asked to pack on his back at the end of his basic training.

American mortars come in two standard sizes, with barrels 81 mm. and 60 mm. in diameter, 3½ inches and 2½ inches respectively. And for each size of mortar, there are two sizes of shells, a long and a short. The long shell for the big mortar weighs about fifteen pounds and contains about six pounds of explosive.

To clarify one point: the mortar is useful not merely because it can be carried to places inaccessible to artillery, but because, being easy to move, its crew can rapidly change the site from which it is firing. Whenever any really dangerous weapon begins firing, the enemy immediately moves to take counteraction. The opening of a battery of mortars is an instant signal to enemy artillery to shell the spot where the fire originated, or to telephone the nearest Luftwaffe to send over a dive bomber. But it will take time for the enemy artillery to find the range, or for the dive bomber to get over. Meanwhile, the mortar will have done its work and can be moved before what's called the counterbattery fire comes down.

You will have a clearer picture of what machine guns are like because they are more often pictured. But you must think of the infantry's automatic rifles and machine guns as a widely assorted lot. The smallest are the stubby little tommy guns that gangsters used to carry and the B.A.R.— the Browning Automatic Rifle—which is the fragile-looking, rifle-sized weapon that has two light legs attached to the barrel. The legs steady the barrel and hold it about a foot above the ground, and the man who is firing it lies on his stomach.

The biggest automatic weapon has a tapered barrel five

feet long and is either an enormous rifle or a miniature automatic cannon, depending on how you look at it. This is the famed American .50-calibre machine gun, whose bullet is a half inch across.

In between these extremes, there is the standard light machine gun, which shoots the same bullet a rifle shoots, these bullets being fed to it in long belts. All these automatic weapons are portable, with the .50-calibre more often found mounted on jeeps and half-tracks or Flying Fortresses. You could not climb a tree in a hurry with the barrel of a .50-calibre machine gun on your back.

The rocket launcher is the first really secret weapon in the war. It was first used in the landing in Africa and only in recent months, very properly, has the army allowed even a reference to it in print. Its mechanism is still secret. But this much the enemy already knows to his regret: that American infantrymen, fighting on foot, now have a weapon with which one man can knock out even a Mark VI tank, if he hits it in the right place.

Close on the heels of the rocket launcher, in ability to throw an explosive charge where it will do the most good, is the grenade thrower, an attachment which makes it possible for a rifle, literally, to shoot a hand grenade instead of a bullet.

All these weapons are infantry weapons, over and above and in addition to the infantry's traditional rifle. The American standard M-1, or Garand, rifle is called a semi-automatic because the soldier doesn't have to work a bolt by hand to reload it. Having put in a clip of eight cartridges, he has simply to pull the trigger eight times to fire all the shots. (If, when he held the trigger down, all eight shots fired in succession, the gun would be a "full automatic.")

Mortars, automatic weapons, rocket launchers, grenades, and rifles—these were the weapons with which "we" were to take the funnel pass northeast of El Guettar. Our tactics were more primitive. The newspaper reader understands that a mountain, or a desert, or a large body of water, is a military obstacle. But what he could learn only on a battlefield is the importance not simply of mountains and deserts but of every little rise and fall of ground, every rock and blade of grass. The study and the intimate knowledge of terrain is the beginning and the end of tactics. Everything to do with the ground, its shape, its contours, its texture, even its color at different hours of the day, affects everything both you and the enemy do and can do.

The two adversaries have the terrain of the battlefield in common. Other things being anywhere near equal, the victory will go to whichever understands the terrain best. The Americans won the opening round of the battle at El Guettar because they understood the possibilities of the terrain better than the enemy did.

The enemy understood the funnel as it was described above. He knew the ease with which it could be defended from frontal attack. Standing in the funnel, the enemy looked at its steep sides rising 1800 feet, in some parts almost vertically, to sharp, jagged peaks. He said to himself: "These sides are no problem, for only mountain goats could climb them. There's only the mouth of the funnel to defend." So the enemy dug his positions and sited his guns and laid his mines and his wire to make the entrance of the funnel impregnable. And in the high peaks on either side he saw only sites for observation posts from which to look a long way off and give warning if the Americans were massing for an attack. What he did not understand was the vulnerability of his position to an attack delivered not at the mouth but in the very neck of the funnel itself. Nor did he know that a way existed by which such an attack might be delivered.

The Americans understood both those facts although neither could be understood from the map alone. Even the largest scale maps showed only rough outlines of the funnel and gave no details of the character of its sides. A surveying party might have worked a year to map the contours of the pass accurately and in detail. Apparently, no surveyor had ever tried to master it, and the contours on the best French map were about as accurate—and no more—as a freehand sketch could make them. The reconnaissance parties of the American Rangers, the scouts and the patrols, had learned the meaning of the rocks and hills first-hand. They had learned them rapidly and accurately in a very few nights, slipping and scrambling up around the edge of the enemy's position. And, as in all good intelligence work, every means of obtaining information had been used. To their own first-hand knowledge, they had added the knowledge of Arab shepherds.

And so, on the day before the attack began, the Americans knew and understood something of which the Germans and the Italians were ignorant—that the north face of the pass they held was broken and cut into a succession of gorges, crevices, saddles and slopes. These twisted and turned, here rising three hundred feet and there dropping two hundred. Linked together they could serve as a path along which men could pass single file.

As the crow flies, the distance was only five miles. Taking ten or twelve, a man could manage it walking in all but one place. There, he would have twenty feet of mountain climbing, but if there were a chain of men, one man could help another.

If the enemy had perceived this fact, he would also have perceived that the whole route could be traversed without once silhouetting a man against the skyline, or exposing him to direct observation from within the pass. And he would have seen that the end of this route came out in a narrow defile just back of the thousand-foot peak which formed the wall of the very narrowest part of the funnel, in other words, directly in the rear of his defensive position.

Knowing these things, the enemy could have foretold his defeat if he ever allowed the Americans to surprise him by coming this circuitous way. Once on the hill over the nar-

rowest part of his position, the Americans would be breathing down the back of his neck. He could not turn to fight
them except at a disadvantage. He would be fighting uphill
and without cover instead of the other way round, as at the
mouth of the funnel.

It is equally true that if the enemy had known these things
he would never have been surprised, for there was hardly a
spot in the long line of march up and down the mountainside
that he could not have defended with a single battery of
machine guns.

The plan of attack was brilliant, but it had also to be delivered brilliantly. It involved the handling of thousands of
men and weapons with delicacy and precision.

Moreover, as you could see at a glance, once you understood the terrain and its problem, the attack had not only to
be delivered as a surprise but it had also to be so sudden and
shocking, so violent and dramatic, that it paralyzed. This was
because, had it been any less than paralyzing, the enemy
might have massed his troops to counterattack, in which event
he would soon neutralize the Americans' hilltop advantage.
For, obviously, while they could get to the hilltop, the
Americans could take no weapons of any size with them and
for what weapons they could carry, they would also have to
carry ammunition. The men defending the valley, then, had
only the ammunition the Americans carried on their backs
to fear, and this would be a quickly expendable item. After
that, they would be as harmless as mountain goats.

The defenders' position at the mouth of the funnel was so
strong that they had never to worry about it and could leave
a dozen men there while they hunted down the wretches who
had the temerity to climb on their backs with only a few
mortar shells and a bandolier of rifle ammunition apiece.

To forestall this possibility, the American attack had to
rely on surprise, shock, and terror—once again like Indians,
they must come with war whoops.

All this was part of the battle plan, foreseen and planned

for. To get there first and to deliver the stunner, there were the Rangers. The Rangers were to attack violently in order to pin the enemy to their dugouts and foxholes. Then the infantry was to follow and finish the job of harrying the enemy out of their holes. The success of the first attack—which would simply tie the enemy down—would achieve the combat team's first mission: to deny the enemy the use of the road through the gap. Thus the flank of the other battle would be protected. The second mission, the capture of the gap itself, would then be only a matter of time and effort. For the enemy positions, immobilized under fire, could be attacked piecemeal, by our infantry, concentrating on one point after another.

The Rangers, on whom so much depended, were a battalion of four or five hundred men organized in five companies. The Rangers are somewhat misunderstood young men. They are thought of as American Commandos. And, as the term Commando is popularly thought of, that would make them specialists in raiding enemy coastal defenses. Actually, they are either more or less than that, depending on the point of view. They are simply specially trained infantrymen, the specialness of their training being its rigorousness. There is nothing that a Commando or a Ranger can do that an infantryman should not be able to do or which many infantrymen are not able to do. But the Ranger can simply do more of it and do it harder because, in the first place, as an individual he volunteered for the job and was chosen not only because he was an exceptionally good physical specimen, but also because emotionally he was an exceptionally aggressive individual. Starting with these assets as an infantryman, the Ranger was given particularly strenuous training and more time than an infantryman gets on night work, besides training in taking care of himself as an individual rather than as a member of a squad. And then, to keep him aggressive, his life was arranged so that he had rather less garrison duty than the average infantryman. To keep him physically fit, he had very much less transportation and characteristically moved from one bivouac to another on foot instead of by truck. And he was kept in special units, his pride in them specially encouraged.

In the end, the Ranger turned out neither a special new kind of soldier—like a paratrooper—nor a superman, as the feature stories would have him, but simply a close approximate to the ideal basic unit of any army—the perfectly trained infantryman, tough and well co-ordinated physically, skillful with any weapon he can carry, an aggressive fellow, conditioned to hate his country's enemies and literally to enjoy killing or capturing them.

More often than not, Rangers are given missions involving the use of no more than a company or two of them. A whole battalion of these young men, with the opening of the battle of El Guettar, were chosen for the mission of finding their way through the mountains by night and shocking the enemy into immobility in the dawn at the end of the march. To the infantry combat team itself was given the mission of following the Rangers and destroying or capturing the enemy they had run to earth.

The Rangers brought company D of the First Engineers Battalion with them because company D had a battery of 81-mm. mortars—and because amongst the combat engineers, who are no sissies, company D had some special reputation for aggressive night reconnaissance. The Rangers themselves had light mortars, 60-mm. The Engineers' 81-mm. mortars were to be the Rangers' heavy artillery.

The last communication D company got from the Rangers' colonel before it shoved off with them was brought by its own Captain Henry. His hell squads squatted on the rocks around him, and behind him the gunners from the half-tracks rested against the heavy parts of the mortars which they were about to shoulder. Even in the moonlight, you could see that Captain Henry was put out about something. He looked his men over a minute before speaking and then said very slowly and in a whisper, but a loud and distinct whisper: "I've just come from Colonel Chittenden of the Rangers, who is now our commanding officer. I want you to know that he only asked me one question. He asked me if I thought you men could keep up with his Rangers. When you get tired, think about that."

3

WHEN you learn to fly there is a tense excitement to the first flight around the field, with a bored instructor telling you what each control does. After that, all is anti-climax until your first solo flight. On your first solo flight, you are proud and frightened and surprised at where you find your self, alone up there in the air with no instructor in the front seat. And after the first solo flight around the field, there are only minor adventures until you decide you know enough about flying to make a cross-country hop; and then, with strange countryside instead of familiar landmarks below you, you are again exhilarated. After you have made your first cross-country hop, you have had the three great experiences which all who learn to fly share. After that you will have adventures but they will be individual experiences in flying, experiences which another flier will understand but which are not universal experiences, are not experiences which you will forever have in common. These three are the memorable experiences of your childhood as a flier.

There are similar emotional high lights in the metamorphosis of civilian into soldier. The first is when you first fire a rifle on a carefully policed range with an instructor at your elbow. The second comes during the first hours of the journey to where the fighting is going on, the hours after you have been given your orders and have taken off—set sail for the theater, climbed into the motor truck which is to take you up to the front or, as in my own experience, sat on a bucket seat in an army transport plane to fly across the line that separates the noncombatant from the combatant. These were the first hours in which I felt committed, as one's life is committed to one's ability to fly on the first solo flight one makes. It is the moment after which one cannot turn back. The third experience comes with the whine of the first bullet that an enemy shoots at you with intent to kill.

Between these emotional experiences there are many others. One feels, one learns, one grows. The emotional development is uneven. They say one learns to iceskate in the summer; perhaps one learns to accept the reality of flying while on the ground. Battle, which is organized disaster, is the more deeply terrifying after it is all over and one is far away from it. The process of accepting strange and unnatural realities is devious and only in their rare climaxes do new experiences seem strange and unnatural while they are happening. Once you have embarked on your first solo flight it is not strange to fly yourself through the air. The flight is wholly real and there are only small and immediate adjustments to make.

It was like that, starting into battle. I did not feel a soldier, sitting in the plane from Algiers with orders which would take me into the line where the battle was. But when the actual march into battle began, I felt neither soldier nor civilian. I do not remember feeling anything but some wonder at the scene around me and a simple and natural interest in finding my place in it, like my wonder at some hitherto unexperienced buoyancy in the air after I had been flying myself for say four or five hours, and interest in applying what I knew of the controls to mastering it.

The scene was complicated. Company D of the Engineers had moved from the rocks where I had left them resting and were forming by the side of the road, straggling in irregular columns. The captain appeared, said "Oh, here you are," and told me to wait with the troops for a runner who would tell me where the Rangers wanted us. He disappeared again. All about in the darkness, officers and men of other units were moving. The runner came purposefully through the crowd and I guessed it was he because he came from the hill where I knew the Rangers were. When he pushed to the edge of the road he stopped and looked uncertainly about him. I asked him if he was looking for the Engineers, and he answered me with authority.

"Colonel Chittenden wants you to bring your men up to the foot of the hill there. You are to follow me and I will show you where."

Both of the platoon lieutenants were with me now. We passed word down the column and set off after the guide, who had not waited for an answer but was disappearing into the crowd. He took us a short way up the side of the hill by the road, motioned to where he wanted us and went off at a trot. When D company got up there, its men fell into their places in columns of squads and I stood on a rock where they could see me and waved at them to sit down because I wanted them to rest until the last minute.

I could look back from where we were and see the slopes and the plain even more clearly. The foreground of the scene was beginning to make sense. From the milling troops near the road, files of men were breaking off and climbing up the slope parallel with the track that we took. Line after line formed and merged and was led up the slope. There was no clue to which unit was which, but these were infantrymen. The units were being sorted and runners were darting from one to the other, trying to find who was where and get word back to their C.O.'s. There were no orders called. The only sounds were still the scraping of feet, the small noises of metal and rock touching and far away the steady throb of many motors running.

The slope was now lined with columns as far as the shadows could be made out clearly, and the men were down off their feet and sitting or lying on the ground again.

I looked up at the hill under which we waited. Now that the moon was higher I could see that the hillside was marked with scores of small burrowings. This was the side of the hill that was away from the enemy and the burrowings were where the Rangers lived. As I watched, they were coming out from dugouts and striking the pup tents that they had set up here and there on scratched-out terraces. The hillside was alive with activity. The Rangers were dropping down out of their bivouac in twos and threes and ones, running rapidly down. When they came to where D company waited, they pushed through and over us. Just beyond us they began their lining up. I thought of men coming out of their barracks for the chow line at home. It seemed the same except there was no horseplay.

Our men carried no packs but the Rangers had light packs attached to their shoulder harnesses. Otherwise, our uniform was like theirs—leggings, trousers, field jacket and helmet. When our men had first climbed from their trucks, the captain had noticed that some of them wore over their trousers the heavy, almost waterproof, ankle-tight overalls that was the bottom half of the armored force battle dress. Most of the engineers had them and wore them in the biting chill of Tunisia's spring. The captain called in the sergeants and said rather sharply, "Tell them to take those things off. Nothing but leggings and trousers. They have a lot of climbing to do"—and the battle overalls had come off and been sent back in one of the trucks.

I stood waiting there, watching the scene of ghostly preparation, of order emerging without orders. In five to ten minutes Captain Henry was back. There was a tall young soldier with him. Instead of a rifle, he had strapped over his shoulder the box with the long rod on it which is the 511 U. S. Signal Corps radio—the walkie-talkie. He held the microphone for it in his hand. The pair came up to me and the captain motioned to the two lieutenants.

"We are to be the third company in the line of march," he said. "Our line of march will be the two hell squads first, and then the mortars. I'll take the head of the column with Ingersoll and you two take your platoons. I want Sergeant Chervassy with me and this is our radio communication with the Rangers. The show starts any minute now."

And then, as a last thought, he motioned to the men for their attention and told them what Colonel Chittenden of the Rangers had said about keeping up.

Even while he was talking, I saw it begin, noticing that the columns nearest us were all on their feet and now first one and then another had begun to move up the hillside back away from the road. Now my only problem would be to avoid losing the captain. Seven hours' acquaintance had convinced me that he was an elusive fellow, given to disappearing without warning. I looked at his silhouette. He was a small, slight man, quick of movement. The best identification, I thought, was the gun on his shoulder. The lieutenant had been right. He carried a weapon the like of which I had not seen before. It had a long thin blue steel barrel, and I could make out only that it took some kind of clip. I said to him:

"If you like, I will keep the sergeant and the radio with me. We'll keep as close to you as we can but you will always know the three of us will be together."

He said, "O.K. Good," and his eye catching some movement in the column nearest us, he was off.

The tall young man with the radio, who had been listening intently, swung in behind me when I followed. The sergeant was already in motion. The columns around us had paid no apparent attention to us but there were whispered orders back and forth now, and as we drew farther up the slopes, the Rangers fell into their marching formation. They marched in two long, wavy lines about fifty feet apart.

Captain Henry was trying to find our place in the flotilla, and while I steered as straight a course as I could, he darted away to whisper to such Ranger officers as he could identify. The Rangers were used to working together at night. They knew each other's sounds and shapes. But our company had never marched with them before and we could not tell who was who. Moreover, the Rangers had a way of starting a march at a pace that would be a jog trot for the average man. First one Ranger company then another drew away from us. You could tell when a company passed for between companies the line would be broken for a space of ten or fifteen feet. The Rangers' junior officers had not apparently heard that they were going to have company on the march. They met Henry's questions blankly with shakes of the head. Finally, the young man with the radio said very respectfully:

"That is E company going by now, sir. It seems likely that would be the last of the column."

Captain Henry said nothing about the lost marching order and we fell in behind E company. The Ranger with the radio continued in charge. He said, again very hesitantly:

"It's the Rangers' custom, sir, to march with half of each squad in each column. That would be half of each of your squads in this column and half in the other."

Captain Henry took a few steps before deciding how to handle this and then, with a shake of his head, motioned me to do something about it. Splitting the squads in half was too complicated. I split the company instead by motioning two platoons out of line and waving them over into the wake of the second Ranger column.

During the time these simple things happened, we were all very busy. The men had been sprawled out, relaxed, and had only a moment's warning to be on their feet. They had their gear to adjust and all of them had then to get in rapid motion in an orderly column. It was immediately apparent—we could not know until that second—that we were to march over neither road nor trail but across country.

Marching across country there meant marching on a hard surface so littered with small and medium pebbles and rocks the size of two or three fists held together that there was nowhere space between them to set a foot firmly on the solid ground. Moreover, the ground beneath these rocks was not level but rising. As it rose, it seemed to weave and tilt from side to side, so that sometimes we walked up a slope and sometimes along one side of a slope and sometimes along the other. The only thing that was constant at the beginning of the march was that at the end of any given ten steps we were several feet higher than we had been at the beginning.

Now, a little over half of the men in the Engineers column, like myself, carried only a rifle, rations, grenades and assorted ammunition, but this equipment was not packed in a carrier which could be ignored. It was stuffed into the bosoms of our field jackets, bulged from the pockets, was draped around the waist and over the shoulders. It would have taken some doing to settle all this gear for a march on a level highway, yet each man for himself had to arrange his gear for walking while moving at a rapid scramble over impossible footing.

The men in the other Engineer squads were, in addition, juggling thirty-five to forty-five-pound pieces of mortars, trying to balance them on their shoulders or get them snug under their arms or find any way they could be held except by sheer power of finger muscles. And for the officers, who also each carried weapons, ammunition, and rations, there were these things to do and some way to find to give comfort or counsel to the men who were having the hardest time of it. Communication was by passing back messages whispered over shoulders. Captain Henry could do nothing but send back word that the men who were not carrying mortar parts should team up with men who were and that each should take turn and turnabout so that no one would have to juggle the mortars continuously.

Meanwhile, I had my own special distraction. Not having had a dress rehearsal, I had not foreseen the flaws in my costume that were presently to develop. My pistol belt was too loose and, weighted down with pistol, ammunition and full canteen, it began to ride on my hips, just where the motion of my legs began. This let the second belt, the one that had nothing but ammunition in it, inch down across my belly until it reached the bottom of the field jacket. As soon as it did so, all the truck that I had stuffed in the front of the field jacket began to jounce, jiggle, squeeze and wedge until first a can of ration and then a heavy grenade and then a stick of candy would come oozing out. This would then force me to hold the whole impending landslide in with one hand. Which in turn threw my shoulders out of line, whereupon the M-1 promptly kited around on its sling and banged me in the back of the helmet.

I knew that I would never be able to regain my place if I stopped for even a few seconds to try to adjust affairs. One was barely able to manage the pace, fresh and untired, because of the treacherous carpet of loose rock. Walk over it one might, with God on his side. Run over it, never—and if one fell behind one would have to run to catch up.

All I could do, stumbling, too breathless even to curse, was to fish wildly in my breast with my one free hand and haul out items and try to stuff them in my already full pockets in such a way that they would stick there. And then laboriously work the top belt up to where it would hold together the walking sack that I had become. And next get some kind of a hitch in the pistol belt. And, finally, get my rifle slung off one shoulder and across to the other, in the hope that it would ride still for a few more steps. Within a hundred and fifty yards I was panting, and I do not remember really ceasing to pant, and breathing simply and normally again, until well after the battle was under way the next morning.

That was the way it was in the beginning of the march: everyone was so busy that time and space were lost completely and there was only the ludicrous motion of tripping and stumbling on, batting oneself in the head with a rifle or the barrel of a mortar and trying to stick things down in overfilled pockets and take hitches in belts.

When the world around me again became reality, the scene had changed just as completely as the scene on the road between the time I had gone forward to the mine field and come back to the start of the attack. When I first got my head up and could look around, having so far seen only Captain Henry's heels and the rocks that rolled from under them to roll in turn under mine, the landscape around us was as bare and desolate as it had been alive and peopled with men when we had begun. There were only the bare sides of the mountains now on both sides of us. The moon that had been bright on the plains and in the foothills had gone. The moon had not really gone, it was we who had moved so deep into the mountains that the moon had not yet risen to where it could shine on us. It was dark and still. Looking ahead, beyond the shiny barrel of Captain Henry's Italian machine gun, I could see only the last two or three of the retreating figures of the company ahead. Behind, after a dozen or so men, there was nothing.

I had my first experience with a sensation that was to recur during the night, a sensation of awakening. I had been so wholly concentrated on keeping my place and my footing—like a man running across a river on logs—that I had become oblivious of everything else. Now, mastering my balance, it was as if I had awakened or come to.

I looked at my watch. It was a little after one. The pace was not as fast as it had been, and the way here was almost level. I noticed that the moonless sky was still clear and perceived that when the moon cleared the mountain tops and shone down on the valley it would be bright again. I thought, "An hour out. We must be about in back of the first Italian wire on the other side of the mountain to the right—just beyond the place I walked out to our mine fields."

I could not judge how long our column was or how far ahead the first man in the Rangers company would be now. It was very still and obviously no one was in trouble yet, for trouble is usually noisy and in these mountains even a small noise would reverberate. I observed that the temperature was ideal for climbing; it was neither too hot nor too cold, but simply fresh and clear. There was no wind where we were down in the bottom of the valley. I thought if I could only see men a few feet ahead, no enemy could see them any farther—but if there were listening posts about, the sighing shuffle of hundreds of feet and the little clickings of the rocks would not be hard to pick up.

I thought, "Good God, nobody can be surprised by this attack!" Only an hour ago I had stood on just a slight rise of ground and the whole plain back there was peopled with live and moving shadows. The movement on that plain must have been visible for miles in the moonlight. I could no longer hear the throbbing of motors on the road back near Gafsa. We were down inside the mountains now. I thought: "Well, I could not hear the motors when we were at the mine field, close to the enemy lines. No, from there I would not be able to see the motion at the Ranger post either."

So there was a chance that the advance had not yet been observed. I remembered the observation planes that had come over at dusk. I thought again that their photographs would show the roads empty and all the division's bivouac of the day before still in place.

I also thought, what the hell do I know about these things. I have never been in a battle before and this is all book talk. This is talk in the mess hall at Camp Edwards about maneuvers. God knows how it happens out here, either better or worse. We never really thought we were hot in camp. We always thought that out in the theater they would do it better—the sentry would never daydream, the communications would always work and our units would always be where and when they were supposed to be—we could see a hundred flaws in everything we did, a hundred ways in which an alert enemy could beat us by capitalizing on our errors. Sometimes we made big talk about what our outfit could do in action but we always knew it was just that.

Well, here I was, marching along behind a real live enemy's line. That wasn't big talk or little talk or any talk at all. That was just happening and it was happening the way it would happen and there was nothing I could do about it except tag along. We were all tagging along, after some battle plan that none of us then understood.

I thought of the rifle that then rested a little easier on my shoulder, and how swell it felt after my good day on the range, the day when the first eleven shots were all bull's-eyes and I would have gone on making bull's-eyes if I hadn't got score fever and grown so tense that I had to take the rifle down from my shoulder, look around and blink my eyes and take long breaths and try to relax between shots. I thought of Jonesy, who was an old soldier and my scorer, lying there next to me on the firing line at the range, so excited by my score that he made me still more nervous, telling me, "Now all you have to do is keep calm." And the lieutenant, who was the range officer, whose shooting I admired very much, walking down the line towards me and saying, "Take your time, take your time." Everyone else had finished shooting except for the rapid fire and down the firing line they were sitting or standing, looking at me and looking out across the range at my target which was the only one in the butts that was up. And then my saying to myself, "Well, it might as well be now," and aiming and seeing the vibration of the barrel of my gun in the sights and knowing that I was now so tense that the trigger squeeze would have to get the bullet in the target—knowing that I would have to catch the movement of the muzzle just as the sights came on the target and squeeze then before the tremble in my left arm had thrown the gun out of line again. And then squeezing and seeing the target go down without either feeling the recoil of the gun or hearing the muzzle blast, I was so anxious about the target. And the target coming up and that second before the marker shows, and then the marker, round and white, over the black bull's-eye. And I had put another in.

And I remembered, at the end of that day, feeling wonderful. I felt that there was nothing as a soldier that I was afraid of because I could shoot straight—and shooting straight is more than just pointing a steel barrel and tripping the hammer with the trigger. It is a feeling so strong and satisfying that it must come in the blood from days when men were hunters. Or maybe Freud could explain it. I remember thinking, marching in from the range that day, after the kidding and the congratulations, "Well, to hell with it, let it blow; I don't care where I go as a soldier. I know I can shoot now."

And now walking in the dark with a rifle like that rifle on my shoulder, towards an enemy that was to be shot, I felt neither afraid nor unafraid. I could think back to that old feeling about a rifle but could not feel it again. It was only walking, walking, walking over loose rock on hard ground and it was purely speculation about how far away the enemy was, or where we were, or what would happen next.

These idle thoughts and lots of others passed the time as we marched. You can think a lot of thoughts marching towards a battle because you are very wide awake, and because your feet are in the rhythm of walking and there's nothing else to do. Later on, when the moon came out and it was very beautiful marching through the mountain, I stopped thinking anything at all and simply enjoyed the scenery.

4

NO ONE will believe how beautiful it was on that march after the moon came out, so beautiful it made you forget about the war. The deep valleys, the jagged peaks, the play of moonlight and shadow in the gorges, the delicate translucent puffs of clouds that drifted slowly across the edge of the moon as it rose higher and arched across the sky—all these were themes in a symphony in gray and silver tones. With each turn through the valley, all the shapes changed and rearranged themselves and made new and stirring patterns. The moonlight reflected from one wall of the chasm to the other and back again and became very, very bright. Going over the saddle of a hill, you could see the line of men for several hundred yards ahead, winding down the hillside, figures in soft silver armor.

Slowly the moon counted off the hours as it crossed the sky. It was after two, it was after three, it was after four. The column no longer moved steadily now but went forward fifteen or twenty minutes and then halted. Something ahead was holding the column up. It was the little halts that saved me. I could feel my feet wearing out and my legs began to ache steadily and what I carried was noticeably heavier. I wanted very much to smoke. The last of the orders passed back through the line was: no smoking and no talking. When we halted, each man dropped where he was. The captain and the tall young man with the radio and I were a group. One of us would take out a stick of candy drops and each of the others would pry one off the top and put it in his mouth. The radio was alive and when everyone was still you could hear a high thin note from its speaker. About three o'clock, one of the lieutenants came stumbling up and whispered to Henry,

"How much farther?"

Henry shook his head and shrugged his shoulders. We had stopped and the lieutenant turned and looked at me. His face was full of concern. I looked at my watch. We had been marching over three hours but I did not think we had covered more than two or two and a half miles in a straight line. He looked so concerned that I whispered, "Half-way, maybe."

The lieutenant looked back at the captain and said, "That's bad, that's very bad. The mortars are too tough for them."

The captain thought a moment and looked ahead into the moonlight. There was a climb and then there was a drop and as far as you could peer through the shadows only more hills, more valleys. The captain sighed and said, "Let them begin dropping back. Pull connecting files from the squad ahead."

Connecting files are soldiers spaced out between elements of a march to keep contact, to relay directions, and show the way.

Then he said to the boy with the radio, "Can you raise Colonel Chittenden?"

The radio man looked at his watch and when he nodded, I knew his little set was still out of the range of the enemy. I guessed, here in the mountains, that might be five miles. He spoke into the microphone. "Henry to Chittenden. Henry to Chittenden. Over."

Instantly the machine answered, "Chittenden to Henry. What is it?"

Henry said, "Let me have the microphone," and whispered into it. "The mortar squads are dropping back, the going is too tough. Connecting files out." And then, "Any instructions? Over."

There was a few seconds' silence on the machine. "Chittenden to Henry. O.K., do the best you can. Over."

The men in the column ahead got to their feet and moved silently away. The column was off again and we marched. Now I walked, watching the ground ahead, playing a game with the ground, trying to outwit it by finding spaces between the stones in which to place each footstep—or if there were no places, flat stones that would not tax my ankles. I could see now that it was going to be a question of how carefully I played that game for there was no reserve strength in my ankles, and if I put my weight on a foot that was not firmly on the ground my ankle would go and that would be the end of it. And I knew, too, that small fractions of ounces of energy would count now. I thought, the top of me will be all right if my feet will get me there. The top of me is not tired.

The thought kept coming back to me that we were well behind the enemy lines now, and were coming close to a place where the slightest slip in the discipline of the march would count. The shuffling whisper of the hundreds of footfalls blended into a monotone. But now and then, somewhere along the column, someone would hit a stone at the wrong angle and it would clatter down the hillside. Or there would be the little tinkle of a rifle barrel tapping a helmet. Then the heads in the column would raise in disapproval or to listen more carefully. Each man in the column was feeling what I was beginning to feel, our nearness to the enemy. I began to be conscious of the blue steel of the barrel of Captain Henry's Italian rifle. It sparkled and glittered in the moonlight. I had been glad I could spot it before so that I could identify the captain in the dark. Now the barrel's brightness annoyed me. A man on one of those peaks who could not see the shadows of the men mingling with the shadows of the rocks would wonder about that flicker of light. The column became quiet; there were long intervals when not even a single stone rolled down. Each man was walking gently, gently.

The halts became more frequent and when it was almost five we sat, breathing heavily after an especially long climb, for many minutes. And then we moved up a few feet and sat again. There was a very heavy shadow just ahead and you could not see where the trail went. When at last we came to the edge of the shadow we saw why the column had been hesitating. There was a real cliff here. The men had to climb down it one by one. The men who were carrying more than their slung rifles had to pass the equipment from hand to hand. When each man went over the cliff he went rapidly, as the man ahead was melting into the darkness under his very eyes. A new fear, the fear of being lost or left behind, seemed to move each man and they went down the cliff as if it were not at the end but at the beginning of five hours of climbing up and down.

Captain Henry seemed as agile as a gazelle. He was gone before I could swing my legs over the edge of the cliff and look to see where I would jump, and brace myself for the jump to a rock three or four feet below, and then to another and another and another. Down at the bottom of the shadow the whole thing seemed to close up, to end against a huge boulder ten or fifteen feet high. Then, as the eyes became accustomed to the darkness there, I could see a crevice under the boulder, down to the right. It was the only opening. I twisted onto my stomach and stuck my legs through it and gradually, holding my weight with my arm, lowered through. My feet touched something, then gave way, and I went down bouncing from rock to rock. And suddenly I was on the flat of a stream bed, quite alone, out of breath and panting.

There was no way to go but along the stream bed. A long way beyond I could see moonlight again and it seemed, from there under the cliff and the big boulder, as bright as sunlight. I ran towards it. The surface of the stream bed felt so flat and firm to feet that had been climbing so long over rocks that it was suddenly as if they had been bathed in cool water. I ran because I had not realized how much it had meant to be one of a column instead of being alone. I wanted to be with the end of the column ahead, and quickly. I did not want to be lost there.

Where the stream bed came into the moonlight I almost collided with a doughboy standing. He whispered tonelessly, as he had whispered to hundreds ahead of me, "Climb to that little shelf there," pointing, "and then curve to the left around the base of the hill and then at the end of the plateau, go down in the valley to the right." And then, as if it could be done, "Keep closed up."

As I turned and left him, our boy with the radio came through and he was running so he collided with the sentry. I motioned him to follow.

After we passed the big drop it went very quickly. The footing was better and they must have been urging the men ahead to move faster. We caught sight of Captain Henry at the far end of the plateau but only for a moment. The radio man stayed by me like a shadow. I didn't see the sergeant again. I was peering ahead always, to find the end of the column and somehow keep in touch and not lose the way. It was a race with the moon now for the moon was across the sky and close to the peaks on our right. There was just the first trace of growing light on the left.

I was almost up to Captain Henry again when, there on a little knoll of grass, we came abruptly to where Colonel Chittenden waited. I knew it was the colonel by the glob of silver on his helmet, and he had another walkie-talkie man with him and two officers. He spoke in a loud whisper and there was a note almost of exultation in it. He spoke as if to old friends, abruptly and without introduction. "Do you realize what we have done, men! Do you realize! We've got five whole columns through!"

There did not seem to be any answer to this. Captain Henry made none. The colonel stepped closer and peered at him, stooping a little to look under the shadow of his helmet. "You're Captain Henry, aren't you? You're the fellow with the engineers." And then, as if coming to from an ecstatic reverie, looking at the watch on his wrist, "We've got to keep going fast now. The attack begins at six. About eight we'll want your mortars, and will you leave out files, Henry, to show the infantry the way? They could get lost in here." Then the colonel's enthusiasm bubbled up again. "You know what this means to them out there, don't you? We've got to get this show under way on time. Their flanks will be wide open if we don't get this show under way on time. But I've got five whole companies past here and they are on up ahead."

Captain Henry continued to stand silently and I stood close by him, panting from the last hour. The colonel and his walkie-talkie and his two officers went off across the knoll of grass and disappeared rapidly. We followed, still not speaking.

After that there were no columns to follow. The Rangers were gone and we were simply coming up as fast as we could. It was well after five, it was five-thirty, it was a quarter to six. Now, the valleys we walked through were well defined and we could not lose our way.

You could not recall the moment it had happened, but the night had passed and it was light, even in the valley. It was fourteen minutes to six, it was twelve minutes to six, it was nine minutes to six. The head of our column had caught up with us and I could recognize the faces of the men of D company. They were expressionless. They looked neither tired nor tense now.

We saw the man who was waiting for us a long way ahead, standing at the top of a jagged pile of rocks. "Colonel Chittenden said to tell Captain Henry to hold his men here. The position's right over this hill"—pointing almost straight up to the right and a little ahead, to the brow of the hill silhouetted sharply against the sky. "Colonel Chittenden said to tell Captain Henry to keep his men down, behind those rocks there."

Captain Henry nodded. The runner turned and went off.

As his men came up, Sergeant Chervassy motioned them down behind the rocks. They went where he pointed and each man, as he found a place for himself, dropped down, taking his rifle from his shoulder and stretching out his legs, laying his rifle across him or putting it on the ground beside him, then lying back against the rocks motionless. It was eight minutes to six, it was seven minutes to six, it was four minutes to six. In ones and twos, more men came up and these, seeing the others resting on the rocks, went there and rested too without being directed. Captain Henry and I stood and looked at the line of the hill against the sky. Chervassy was ahead of us. He had gone down on one knee and was resting on it, with the butt end of his rifle on the ground.

Almost as one man all three of us saw it and the sergeant flung out one arm pointing and turned his head back towards us, shaking it violently up and down. There was something moving on the top of the hill there. And all three of us held our rifles as if a clay pigeon were about to go up and we must be alert to shoot it quickly. I got my finger inside the guard of the rifle and pressed the safety off. It was a man, all right, on the hilltop, and now another and another. Each was doing something purposeful, running a little way, crouching, dropping out of our sight. The figures were too small and black for us to see more than that they were men. At that second I was not tired and I could not feel my body at all. I felt very wideawake and alert. Then, as we watched, we could see below the figures on the skyline other figures climbing towards them. We had not been able to make them out before but these unmistakably wore khaki and we could see the shape of their helmets against the gray of the hillside. We put down our rifles.

I looked up at the sky and it was quite light. I remembered suddenly how much I had wanted to smoke and I found the cigarettes in my pocket and lit one. It was four minutes after six. It was very still in the dawnlight. Some of the men who had come up and were resting under the rocks were already asleep in these few moments. They would rest there or sleep till they were told what was wanted of them next.

Then in the stillness, like a perfect accent to it, there came, clearly and each note perfect, the sound of a bugle call. It came up from beyond where the men were silhouetted against the skyline, and it echoed once or twice in the valley where we were and then, before the sound was over, the shooting began, up there and over near where the sounds of the bugle came from. Captain Henry looked at me and I looked at him, and said, "Come on, let's go up there and see what's cooking." He said to the sergeant, "Give me two men for runners and wait here until I send for you. Keep the men together."

5

WHEN Captain Henry and I reached the top of the hill
the battle had been on for fifteen or twenty minutes. Scrambling up the hillside, we had heard first rifle fire and then the
heavy coughing of a machine gun, and finally a succession
of explosions. All the sounds came from beyond the hill, and
climbing the hill I suddenly thought it was like hurrying,
out of breath, up the ramp of a football stadium with the
sound of cheering from inside, knowing that the game has
begun and that something exciting has happened but not
knowing what it is and being excited and impatient. The only
things I remember, climbing the hill, are the sounds of the
firing and that feeling of excitement and wanting to get
quickly to where I could see what was happening. For the
moment I ceased being a soldier and turned journalist.

At the top of the climb, where we had first seen the
Rangers silhouetted against the skyline, we found not a peak
but an oblong plateau, bowl-shaped, higher at the edges than
in the center. It stretched for the length of several city blocks,
parallel to the ridge line of the higher mountains and therefore also parallel to the road through the pass. The plateau
was about a block wide. Like the valley, the ground on it
was hard and rocky but my first impression was of the flowers there, the flowers and the birds. The little hilltop, for all
the dryness of its ground, was a meadow of flowers, daisies
and little pink and purple and white flowers, ankle-high.
There were many small birds in the air and, excited by the

gun fire, they swooped and turned. To the left, at the far end of the plateau, the ground rose another few hundred feet and ended in a rounded knob of rock. There I could see a group of American officers and men sitting on the rock and looking through glasses across the plateau to something beyond it.

All along the side of the plateau towards the enemy, there were big rocks quite close together like a roughly made stone fence. Behind each crouched a doughboy. It was the firing line, and as we walked across the plateau first one man and then another would raise his rifle and steady it on the rock, or lying down place his rifle alongside a boulder, and fire a shot. The rifles cracked and popped almost continuously. Back from the firing line, perhaps ten or fifteen feet below it, there was another line of soldiers. These were on their backs or their faces, their rifles alongside them or under their heads, and they all seemed to be sleeping peacefully. But for their helmets, the men on the firing line, from the postures they took, might have been from a print of the Civil War, and they behind a tumbledown stone fence in Virginia instead of Tunisia. The scene was very orderly and undangerous-looking. Still, I carried my rifle in front of me in both hands, expectantly.

I crossed the plateau diagonally toward the center, to where the most firing was going on. I remember I had passed the sleeping soldiers and had begun to crouch down when the first enemy bullet came by. It came ricocheting off one of the rocks ahead of me and zinged with that high snarling whine that only a ricocheting bullet can achieve. Then there was another and another and, keeping time with the bullets, the deep hollow bark of the muzzle blast of an automatic weapon of some size. It was a big machine gun firing from a position on the other side of the road. My head came down fast and I dropped down beside a doughboy who was just aiming his rifle. I inched up alongside him and looked out.

We were on the rim of one side of a valley whose walls

made an almost perfect V. At the bottom of the V it was flat for only a small space, just wide enough to hold the road, which ran straight. The road was deserted and there was no sign of life anywhere, not on either hillside or on the flat. There were two road blocks on the road, one to the right and one to the left. Each consisted of two heavy walls of stone set so that a vehicle would have to wind through them in an S. The scene in the valley looked even more peaceful than the scene on the hilltop. I couldn't see any enemy at all.

I could hear the firing around me and every few minutes there was the deep chugging of the gun across the valley but I could not find it. I could at first see nothing at all. Then gradually, as I peered, I could make out on the mottled brown-gray of the hillside, spots of lighter brown. Looking still more carefully I could recognize that they were positions of some kind—here, sandbags made an unnaturally straight line; there, there was the loose dirt that had come from some excavation. While I watched, the first mortar fired, one of the Ranger's light mortars from the plateau behind me.

I had never heard a mortar fired before and the noise quite close made me jump. A mortar makes a terrific noise when it fires, a big heavy belching noise. Not knowing what it was that had made the noise, I was surprised again—it seemed minutes later—when there was an explosion down in the valley on the other side of the road—a flash and light gray smoke widening from it. That was the mortar shell landing. The mortar fired again and again, and after the third or fourth shot I had diagnosed the sound and it ceased to make me jump.

The rifleman next to me fired slowly and methodically, looking out between each shot as if he could see where his bullets were landing. I thought he was firing at a strong point near where the mortar shells were landing, but it was too far away to see the kick of dirt from a rifle bullet. I was still much too interested to do any shooting on my own. I wanted to take the scene apart and find out what was happening.

Now turning my head first one way and then the other I

could orient the valley. To the right it widened steadily and the hills grew lower and, perhaps a mile from where I was, the plain began. That was the mouth of the funnel. There I could see another road block and the aprons of barbed wire, very neatly and carefully patterned. They ran high up into the foothills and there were two of them, two bands. I could follow the road past the wire and, just visible in the distance, I could make out the fork where I had been the night before.

From the fork I could follow the other road, the one that led to Gabes. It ran across the mouth of the funnel and then past the end of the hills opposite, disappearing behind them. Far beyond this road, shining in the early morning light, there was the dead-white flat of the salt lake there.

Looking back to the fork again, I could make out that just beyond it and spread across the plain, there were the black dots that could only be vehicles. Now, looking at them, I could notice little flashes coming from some of them. That would be the vehicles of the other combat team, advancing across the plain. The dots seemed to be moving, but very slowly. They were in no formation that could be recognized but the front line of the field of them was a well-defined line.

As I watched, something caught my eye far beyond the vehicles out on the plain. It was a succession of little puffs of smoke. The cannon in the vehicles were firing and those were shells bursting on enemy positions further out on the plain. The little puffs of smoke were gray and hung above the ground for only a moment and then dissolved. The puffs of the shells were on the right or the far side of the road. Sometimes they came singly and sometimes all at once there would be a dozen or more of them. The sounds from them could not be heard above the noise of the rifles crackling around me.

Suddenly, on the near side of the Gabes road, right where it passed the point of the mountains opposite, there was a little ball of white cotton, growing rapidly, as in a nightmare, billowing from a puff of cotton into a small white cloud and the clouds streaming out to the right of where the ball of cotton had been. Then there was another ball of cotton and another cloud streaming. I did not know what this phenomenon meant. Now there came four puffs of white at once, and the clouds that grew from them ran together and I thought it must be the laying of a smoke screen. It was not. The white puffs were the bursts of shells from the 105-mm. howitzers. The battery was using shells which burst with a white smoke so that the fire might be more easily followed. They were shelling the point of the mountain, groping to find a position that looked down on and commanded the road. All this was going on on my right, beyond where the valley widened.

To the left of where I lay, the walls of the valley closed in on the road and the narrow neck of the valley was just opposite the far end of the plateau. Turning this way, I could see the side of the hill rising to the plateau I was on. I could then look on up to the officers on the peak which commanded the whole scene. And as I watched, things began to happen on the hillside—sharp explosions, shattering sounds quite unlike the hollow BOO! noise the mortars made. And with each explosion there was a scattering of rock, fan-shaped, and thin dirty smoke. Explosions followed one another and after each the smoke hung higher up along the slope of the hill. The last two of a succession of explosions were, one on the plateau just beyond where we lay, and the other on the side of the pinnacle, just under where the officers waited. With the last two sounds the soldier next to me was flat down on his belly behind the rock. And so was I. I didn't need a lecture to tell me that these were enemy shell bursts and that they were walking up the hill as the enemy gunner lengthened the range. They were after the command post that was still silhouetted sharply above the rock.

The face of the soldier next to me was very close to mine. He said in a conversational tone, "There are two squads down after that baby. It's an eighty-eight. It's over just behind the point—you know, the narrow place there."

The shell bursts were a good city block from us, and I do not remember being frightened then but only confused about what would happen next. What happened next was that the gun stopped firing. When no shells came for several minutes, the soldier next to me got on to his knees and looked up the valley towards the narrow part. "Yeh, they must have got it all right," he said, still in a conversational tone.

Another bullet ricocheted off the rocks below us. It had a different sound from the other bullets, a higher, lighter sound. The soldier with me stopped being conversational. He said sharply, "That's a God-damn sniper. God damn, I hate snipers. Now where's that son-of-a-bitch?"

I came up alongside the soldier and we both looked, holding our rifles near our shoulders. We looked down the hillside dropping away from us, trying to let the brown rocks and the gray ground and the patches of sparkling color that were flowers make a pattern that would be a background against which we could see anything foreign to the countryside, or anything moving. We could see nothing but rocks. Neither the soldier nor I fired because we could find no target.

The firing he had been doing across the valley had been covering fire. He had been firing at points too far away for accuracy, simply to make the enemy cautious about coming out or sticking their heads up. He had been keeping the enemy heads down in exactly the way the sniper and the machine gun outfit were keeping our heads down.

A soldier ran along behind us, crouching, and called to the man next to me. He simply said, "Come on," and the man next to me backed away from the rock until he was far enough down the bowl of the plateau so that when he stood up straight his head would still be below the line of fire from the valley over the parapet. Then he turned and ran after the other soldier. All along the line every third or fourth man was backing out and going down to where he could stand and run, crouching. There was a company on the ridge and one squad was being called out for some mission.

Suddenly, a few hundred yards beyond me, the soldier who had brought the other soldiers together made a single motion with his arm, waving it forwards toward the wall. The ten or twelve soldiers who were abreast of him each ran back up to the wall and through gaps in it and were off down the side of the hill. I watched them fascinated. They were running down the hill as we used to run in skirmishes at Camp Edwards, each running with his rifle held high in front of him, zigzagging half a dozen steps and then going down flat on his face in a crevice or behind a rock. They were after the sniper.

After the first two rushes they did not seem in any hurry. They would lie still and peer intently ahead for minutes at a time and then first one and then another would suddenly be on his feet, leaping down from rock to rock. They strung out over a wide area and you could not see the whole line at one glance but had to look from man to man to follow how they were going. The slope of the hillside was uneven and a few hundred yards beyond, one by one, they disappeared from sight.

The men who were still behind the stone wall where I was paid no attention to the skirmish line but kept on firing across the valley. The hunters did not return. Presently, there were rifle shots from where they had gone but you could only presume that it was they and not the enemy firing.

I do not know how long I lay watching all this, or when the intense excitement of the scene began to wear off. When I was first there, there seemed no time. Now I suddenly realized that there was something the matter with my leg. I tried to move it and found it bound in cramps. I drew back from the wall, crawling, and found I was so stiff that even moving my whole leg a little was a great effort. I crawled down from the line and took stock. I rubbed and pounded the calf of my leg until the pain of the cramps stopped. I was going to be a hell of a help to D company if I couldn't walk. I had forgotten all about D company, watching the battle begin, and now I felt guilty of misbehavior.

Looking around me, I saw Captain Henry and his radio operator, sitting with their backs against a rock. Around him, sprawled on the ground, some with their helmets over their eyes and some with the helmets like pillows under their heads, were men of D company, waiting. The Ranger company that had been there was still sleeping just behind the firing line, waiting for its turn to come to go into action. Waiting, and like good soldiers, resting.

When I came up to Captain Henry he said "hello" as if I were just back from a stroll in the park after breakfast. I sat down beside him and we talked a little about what was going on—about where the various sounds of fire were coming from and what sound was from what weapon. Captain Henry looked a little worn but the young man with the radio seemed fresh as a daisy. He had a long, smooth-shaven face and there was an air of quiet alertness about him. Captain Henry was waiting for the men with the mortars to come up, and for the radio to tell him where they were wanted and what targets they should fire on. Until the mortars came up, there was nothing for the engineers to do but wait with the Ranger companies that were being held in reserve.

Without warning, the radio began to talk. It said clearly and distinctly, "Chittenden to C company, Chittenden to C company. We need a little bayonet work, we need a little bayonet work. Report to Lieutenant ——" I could not catch his name—"Chittenden to C company. Do you hear me? Do you hear me? Over."

And then, in another tone of voice, the radio said, "C company to Chittenden, C company to Chittenden. Coming up, sir. Coming up. Over."

As we sat there, the line of Rangers who had been sleeping came to life. The men scrambled to their feet, shaking the sleep out of their heads and some of them rubbing fists in their eyes like sleepy children. And each of them reached backward and loosened the bayonet that hung there, taking it out of the scabbard and fixing it on the end of his rifle as he walked and shook himself awake. The men who were going to make the bayonet charge walked off in a line to the left of where we were and we could see the head of the column lead it down around the back side of the hill on which the officers still sat, silhouetted against the sky. The men at the rear end of the line were passing within a few feet of us. In these few seconds they were wide awake and some of the men on the firing line who had turned, watching them pass, were kidding them.

"Bring 'em back alive, big boy," one of them yelled.

"Bring 'em back alive, nuts!" said someone in the column.

"You tell him, pal," another man yelled.

The head of the line was going faster and the men began to run to catch up. As the last one passed, one of the men in the firing line said to another, "I bet they don't bring them bastards back alive. I bet they kill them bastards. They don't like not to kill them bastards. You wait and see, they won't bring no prisoners back."

Half an hour later we heard the charge, and running stiffly to the rampart again, I could see the end of it. It was against a point almost opposite us. The Ranger company had gone down around the far end of the hill and must have passed below us, behind a ridge which gave them some cover just this side of the road. And then they must have charged across the road and there was no cover at all there. When I found them, they were close to what it was they were attacking, and it did not seem to be firing back. The men were in a semicircle on their feet and going in. The noise, even heard a rifle-shot away, was stunning. You could not pick the sounds apart. It was like a continuous, rippling explosion. It was the fire of tommy guns and rifles and the explosions of the grenades the men were throwing ahead of them. Down in the bottom of the valley, where they were, the echoes of these sounds rolled into one continuous crackling roar.

I could make out the parapet of the enemy's position now. It was notched into the side of the hill. Then, as they closed in, a little blob of white came up over the parapet and waved frantically back and forth. A loud clear voice at my elbow said, "Stay where you are, stay where you are, stop right there." The man with the radio had come up after me and Colonel Chittenden's voice was coming out of it. "Don't go in after them. C company there, you there, don't go in after them. Make them come out to you." And then, as the firing stopped and the echoes rolled away and each roll of the echo was fainter, I saw the men who had made the charge freeze in their tracks.

There was a little wait. The only movement beyond the road was the waving of the little white symbol of surrender. And then running, scrambling, trying to keep its footing and its balance with its little hands in the air, a tiny gray figure coming down towards where the doughboys waited. And then another and another. "Four, five, six," someone near me counted. Everyone along the firing line had stopped firing and was watching. I thought, will they be Germans or Italians? There was no way of telling so far away. We had not been sure the night before who would be there when we attacked.

I looked at my watch. I felt as if I had been on that hilltop for a long weekend. It was a few minutes after eight o'clock in the morning.

6

I THINK there must come to every soldier, during his first battle, a moment when he looks around and says to himself, "Is this all there is to a battle?"

This generation, at least, has been brought up on the novels and the histories of the last war which told of weeks in the trenches under continuous fire, of 36-hour barrages and "going over the top," of mass charges to cut your way through wire while enemy bullets burned around you. Maybe it was like that all the time—I was still in a training camp then—or maybe it was like my first battle and the other battles in this war that I learned of first-hand from the men who had fought in them. Nothing could be more violent than the most violent moments, but these moments were spaced out. Between them there were long spells of waiting, walking, and waiting.

The Stukas that attacked us in the afternoon were to give us one violent experience. Two days later, when the Tenth Panzer Division attacked at El Guettar, there were twelve continuous hours of firing as fast as the ammunition could be brought up and the whole American position was under almost continuous bombardment from the enemy. On the day after that, one American infantry battalion was cut off on a hilltop, the same kind of a hilltop where we found ourselves that first morning. After the Americans had fired all their ammunition, there was nothing left for them but to lie in the foxholes they had dug, where most of them were presently shelled into insensibility and then captured when a German shock regiment charged up the hill in the moon-light. The very few survivors told of it. The men I was with had been at Kasserine Pass, and they would still marvel, sitting around after chow and chewing the rag, at the amazing precision of German artillery fire—how it seemed to seek out each individual mortar, each machine gun, and how each of the first few succeeding shells burst closer until the men could not work the weapon but had to lie still on the ground, each man saying to himself, "Well, if it's a direct hit I won't ever know it," and scared cold and clammy and wishing to God only that it would stop.

These violent moments are very violent and they are what you read of in the cables from the front because why should a correspondent waste his employer's money at a dollar a word to tell of the hours of waiting on a battlefield that the soldier remembers because he was so hungry, or of marches he recalls because his feet hurt so. Yet, marching and waiting are what battles are made of—for the soldiers and the junior officers who do the fighting in them. The killing and the getting killed are the punctuation marks between long sentences of waiting and marching, marching and waiting, eating as best you can, sleeping in snatches wherever you are, and each man trying to keep a running track of the score simply to know where he is and what may be expected of him next.

All through the long hours of that first day at El Guettar —and looking back, each hour seemed a full day long—it was like that. After the excitement of the first contact, the first sound and sight of enemy fire, the first shell bursts and the ricocheting bullets, it was a day of waiting in the sun and watching, punctuated by sudden bursts of action when one's turn to act came. It is not surprising when you stop to think of it, and only surprising when you are there because somehow you didn't think it would be like that. A runner cannot sprint at top speed much more than one hundred yards. Of the thousands of men engaged in even a small battle most of them always are waiting, resting or simply moving from one place to another. Only a few at any given hour are engaged in climax action. The Ranger squads that made the first bayonet charge I saw had been asleep a few minutes before it began, and a few hours later they were sprawled on the ground again, smoking and opening cans of rations and dozing off again, for by noon they had not really slept for thirty hours.

In the imagination of every soldier who expects to fight, the word "battle" grows until he expects the real thing to call for continuous heroism, unbelievable fortitude and a superman's skill at arms. He is just a little surprised then, when he finds that so much of a battle is no more strenuous than the maneuvers he's been on—no more strenuous and much more relaxing, for the sergeants do not yell at him in a battle, nor, when he is taking a quick snooze, does anyone prod him to his feet just for the sake of being sure he is awake. The officers and the non-coms will be awake but their job is to use their field glasses and their wits—no major is going to jump them for having their field jackets unbuttoned or enquire abruptly why the mess account was ten dollars out the week before.

By 8:30 in the morning at El Guettar, a few yards from the C.O. and his radio—so that the body would be there if he wished to recall it to life—I was flat on my back, my head on a stone and my helmet canted forward to shade my eyes, peacefully, deliciously, and blissfully asleep. This process I repeated in fifteen or twenty minute takes throughout the day. Between naps, there continued to be plenty to see and a few jobs to be done.

When 8 o'clock was an hour past and our mortars still had not come, I picked out the men who looked least weary, roused them and took them back with me to find the lost squad. I sent runners ahead to find out where they were and waited on a hillside where I could see any signals that might be relayed to me from the plateau in case any new orders came through from the colonel of the Rangers. When the men with the mortars came winding up through the valley, I had some of them shift loads to men who looked fresher— it had been a grueling climb for them with the heavy, clumsy loads—and led them by the shortest route back to the company commander. Captain Henry was on his feet waving to us when we came in view.

Attacking up the valley, taking first one strong point and then another, the Rangers had at last been stopped at one well-fortified machine gun nest. They had no more ammunition for their own mortars. They had let go everything in the first hours and while they had been successful in pinning the enemy in each strong point to the ground and keeping them from forming for a counterattack, the Rangers had yet to reach the enemy reserves who were in dugouts some way beyond the post that was now holding up the advance.

"Chittenden to Henry, Chittenden to Henry"—the radio kept calling for the engineers' mortars, specifying where they should be set up. We came stumbling across the plateau at a trot. We took the mortars to the far end of the plateau and set one up in a hollow where its crew were safe from rifle and machine gun fire. While the men set the plate on the ground and fastened and adjusted the barrel, Captain Henry and I crawled out on the brow of the hill, each on an opposite side, to where we could look forward to the enemy's post and back to the mortar, so that we could shout back word of where our shells were falling.

It was a good show, right out of the textbook. The mortar was ready, I heard Henry call out his estimate of the range and looked back over my shoulder to see one of the men by the mortar pick up a fat yellow bomb, brace one foot on the metal plate which supported the mortar and, with a quick darting motion, slam the bomb into the muzzle, fins first. Almost instantly there was a terrific bang, with a swishing noise in the echo. I snapped my head back to watch where the shell fell. Nothing happened for what seemed to be a very long time. It was time enough for several of the Ranger sergeants, who had been resting on the hilltop, to climb down alongside me. They carried field glasses on straps around their necks, and were adjusting the eye pieces. From down below me, short of and to the left of the machine gun nest, there was the familiar sharper bang and I saw flying stones and light gray smoke as the mortar shell burst. It was on the other side of the hill from Captain Henry so I cupped my hands and yelled, "Seven o'clock and a hundred yards short."

I had never directed mortar fire but that was the way I would have marked a shot on a rifle range and I thought it would do. From his side of the hill, Captain Henry ordered a correction and yelled for one round. Bang, another shell went. It was still a little to the left but much closer. The third burst seemed right alongside the target and must have scattered stones over it.

The first three rounds, to find the range, had been of the small shells. Now Captain Henry ordered the larger charges. There was again the bang, the wait and the second bang. There was a gusty crosswind blowing down the valley and the first of the bigger shells hit further away from the target. Its explosion was visibly greater. Whoever was in that machine gun nest now knew that the jig was up—that sooner or later we would get a direct hit. We sent two more rounds in quick succession. And then again, up came the white rag on the end of a rifle. On the radio, as I came back to within earshot, "Chittenden to Henry, Chittenden to Henry, nice work, nice work. Over."

It was as easy as that when you had the drop on the enemy and no batteries counterfiring. It had been the first hour of the attack that had really counted—the complete surprise, the ferocity of the first squad rushes. The enemy had no way of knowing that we were only a few hundred men there on the hill. So violent and continuous had been the attack during the first hour that the enemy had been kept under cover. There, sitting on his hilltop, the colonel had been able to direct the attack, to force the surrender of first one point and then another. Presently, the combat team that was to take over began winding up the valley we had traversed and was passing back of the hill to attack beyond. And now our own artillery opened fire.

The first guns to fire were reaching for enemy head-quarters a few miles beyond us. They were 155's. On the hilltop we could see neither the guns, sited far back on the plain, nor the bursting of the shells beyond the next row of hills. We could hear only the eerie whir of the steel as it flew overhead—directly overhead, invisible. The shells seemed to be going very, very slowly. They took a full minute to arc the ten miles through the sky. You could feel the vibration of the air before you could identify any sound. It grew and while it was coming toward you seemed to gather momentum slowly. Then *whoosh!* It was overhead and passing, and the sounds were going away and the vibra-tion dissolving in the air. Finally, *bang!* The noise of the shell came back and echoed from mountainside to mountain-side three or four times before it died away.

At the time the big guns started firing there were several enemy strong points still in business on the opposite side of the road from us, higher up on the hillside than the ones that had already been captured, and harder to surround. About mid-morning a battery of 105's began to work on them. The battery was firing high explosive shells and from much closer than the 155's. The shells' trajectory was lower and we could not hear them come into the valley. The bursts on the slope were like giant handfuls of gravel, flung viciously and spitefully. They made practically no smoke and left craters that were no more than scratches. The shells came very quickly, one after another. They landed just beyond the Rangers' skirmish line.

All this activity I watched between naps, awakening to climb back to the brow of the hill where I could watch it. I also heard most of it on the radio. Once the action had begun and radio silence had been broken, the radios were talking almost continuously. The whole battle was wired for sound. Like ours, each company had its own walkie-talkie and all were on an open circuit with the commanding officer. No one used code—there was no longer any point in secrecy.

Most of the radioed messages were in the highly styled dialogue that radio discipline demands. When the going was hot, however, the colonel of the Rangers used his radio to urge, encourage, exhort, and praise. When the Rangers' mortars were firing, he would chant, "Nice shooting, nice shooting, now faster. Blister them. Give it to them. Another like that and you've got 'em." On different parts of the battlefield there were three or four bayonet charges during the day. When he ordered a bayonet charge, the colonel's voice was calmer and he would say something like, "I think we need a little cold steel over there on the hill mass to the south. Lieutenant, see what you can do for them. I think they are making a nuisance of themselves up there. They are wasting our time. Get them out of there with that steel. We can't fool around here all day." When things weren't going to suit him he'd say, "What's going on around here, anyway? Where's that fire coming from? Doesn't anybody know what's happening in this battle? Who's that down there, beyond the road? That's not you, is it, lieutenant? Will somebody please try to find out what's going on around here."

From time to time the colonel would relay the résumé of what was going on around there back to division headquarters. The résumés were as cheerful as they had a right to be. "Tell them it's going fine. Tell them we control the pass now but that there's a lot of mopping up to do. They could get in here now. But tell them to wait until we've rounded the whole bunch up so that nobody gets hurt."

The first time I visited the colonel's command post was to see the first batch of prisoners that had been rounded up. Not until they had marched the long way round the back of the hill and climbed almost to us could I see that they were Italians. There were six of them in the first lot, and one Ranger doughboy with a rifle was bringing them up to be questioned. They wore woolen caps and long overcoats which came down to their ankles. The overcoats were of heavy material but they were almost in rags, patched or sewn together with coarse, heavy thread or twine.

When I walked over to them, the first man on the line, who must have recognized that I was an officer, stopped and took out a package of cigarettes and offered me one. I thought, "Man bites dog—it's supposed to be the other way round." The Italian was twenty-two or twenty-three years old, a fair-haired boy with a beard of light fuzz. All the others were about the same age but were dark and looked more like Italians. They wore no insignia except two little tin stars, one on each lapel of their overcoats. The dough-boy with them grinned at me and said, "Them and their lousy cigarettes. The colonel said he wanted to talk to 'em up there."

I fell in with the doughboy and the prisoners climbed ahead of us around the back of the rock on which the command post stood and up to it. There was a British padre there with a Commando insignia on his shoulder. I had not seen him the night before. He took charge of the prisoners and sat them in a semicircle around him and spoke cheerfully to them in Italian. He asked them for their papers and scratching into their pockets each man produced a little pile an inch or two thick; identification books, letters, photographs, money. The padre took them and piled them in a heap next to him. "For your intelligence officer," he explained, as I watched him.

The colonel was a few feet away and higher up, on top of the rock. He was looking down the valley through glasses and from time to time he asked the padre to ask the prisoners something—their outfit, where the Germans were, where they had come from and how long they had been there.

The Italian prisoners at first seemed very anxious to please. They were from the Centaurian Division and they had been in Africa a long time and fought through several campaigns in Cyrenaica. The Germans had pulled out forty-eight hours before, taking all the Italians' trucks with them, even the wheels from their cannon. The Italians had no choice but to stay.

When he heard this, Chittenden put down his glasses and said to the padre, "Tell them if they want to send two men back to their own lines it's O.K. with me. Tell them they can go back and tell their friends to call off this nonsense. Tell 'em to tell them that if they don't quit now somebody may get hurt."

The padre set to work translating this. And as he talked the men looked at each other. Three or four of them seemed responsive. But the eldest, who had a black Van Dyke beard and was better kept than the others, scowled. The padre talked some more. Finally, he shrugged his shoulders and said to Chittenden, "I think some of them would like to, but they are afraid of that one there for some reason."

One of the Italians, who had said nothing up to now, suddenly reached out for the pile of papers. He had been the last to turn his papers in and they lay there, several small snapshots on top. The padre spoke sharply to him and he began to cry, mumbling and wiping his eyes with his hands. He was the blond boy with a round face, the one who had offered me the cigarette. The padre picked up the snapshots on the pile of papers, looked at them and handed them to the man who was crying. "What's the matter now?" said Chittenden.

The padre smiled. "He's worried about his mother. Says she won't know whether he has been killed and he wants her picture back." He was the only sad one in the group. He missed his mother very much.

It's an odd sensation, looking at men who have just been shooting at you. I did not feel angry with them, only curious about what they were like. I had seen no one killed or injured yet.

I left the prisoners and climbed up to where Colonel Chittenden was. He nodded to me and smiled. "Well, how are my fighting engineers today?"

I said, "They haven't had much fighting to do, Colonel. Your boys have put on the whole show."

"They *are* an aggressive lot of young men, aren't they?"

They were more than aggressive. The Rangers fought so skillfully that it was past noon before they had their first casualty. The men who came up to the command post to report the success of another bayonet charge told the skipper about it. The Italian machine gunners had been kept down behind their breastworks until the first of the doughboys was only a few feet away. Then two of the Italians stuck their heads up and threw hand grenades at him at once. The first he kicked out of his way and the second he batted with his hand—his left hand, for he had a tommy gun in his right. This second grenade had gone off in the air and fragments of it had torn the doughboy's arm. Colonel Chittenden was solicitous but they told him it wasn't bad.

Colonel Chittenden was a careful commander and on the radio he was continually advising his men on the safest route to get to where they could fire on the enemy, cautioning them to keep down. He kept the battle going, giving the enemy no time to catch his breath, but he was very careful of his men.

It was about two o'clock in the afternoon when he reported to Division that the whole valley could be considered in our hands. From the rock, we could see jeeps and half-tracks a mile or so beyond the mouth of the valley, waiting. The colonel asked that word be sent to them to hold them where they were until the last sniper had been cleared from the valley. "No need for anybody to risk getting shot now," he said to me.

Then the colonel told me to tell Captain Henry that in another hour or two he would be ready for the engineers to go down the hill to pick up the Italian mine fields. I thought, we haven't any mine-detecting equipment with us but it won't take long to go back and get some.

Before I left the command post, I took a last look over the scene. The little dots that were the vehicles advancing down the Gabes road had inched and edged from the horizon on the right to almost out of view on the left. All through the day, at intervals, I had watched them edge forward. There were times when you could see they had been very busy. For an hour or more enemy shells were bursting over and amongst them. There were some big salvos when a dozen or more shells were exploding at once. You could see the gray smoke from the enemy shells bursting amongst the American vehicles, and the white smoke of our own 155's continued to drift over the enemy's position. After the first two or three shots, the American batteries fired in volleys of four shells which burst close to each other in a line. The fire moved from point to point, hunting targets.

In the middle of the morning, the JU-88's had come. The standard air raid warning at the front is three short blasts on a whistle. No one had even whistled an alarm where we were because they obviously were headed for the other battle. There were a dozen or more of the enemy ships, two-motored bombers looking, in the distance, not greatly different from transport planes over La Guardia field, except that they were flying in a compact formation. There were as many Messerschmitts again in the air over them, several thousand feet higher. The flying of the fighter planes was fascinating in its intricacy. They turned endlessly, weaving in and out of each other's path. Presumably this was S.O.P.— standard operating procedure—by which they made themselves difficult targets from the ground. Another reason for their banking and turning was to enable the pilots to look in all directions of the compass, and above and behind the formation, so that no attack could surprise them.

When they were still some distance from the American forces, the bombers broke their formation and they, too, began weaving and twisting. It was magnificent flying, skillful and daring. It was daring because they flew so low and because the forces on the ground were ready for them. The whole plain sparkled with the flashes of cannon and heavy machine guns and even from where we were it sounded like the 4th of July. The puffs from the ack-ack shells began bursting in front, above, below and in the midst of the German formation, hundreds of little puffs of dark gray. The Germans flew right through it.

As they came on over the target, on the hilltop where we were everything stopped and the soldiers who were asleep awakened, and all of us gaped in silence. That old feeling that I remembered so well from London and Chungking and Moscow came back to me, that desperate aching wish to see them knocked down out of the sky. The firing on the plain seemed to double in volume.

It was all over in thirty seconds. Still twisting, still weaving, both layers of planes swung in a great arc away from the battlefield and away from us and circled the edge of the plain out over the salt lake in the distance and then were gone. In the afternoon they came again but only twice. It was not until the next day that I heard the score—two 155-mm. cannon knocked out and nine prime movers wrecked. No one had the exact count on the casualties. They had been heavy, heavier than the casualties from the shelling had been. But the advance had gone on and it had covered five or six miles by afternoon.

Our own valley was alive with American soldiers now. The infantry had long since caught up and they were making sure the ground was clear by walking up one hillside and down the next in long close lines of skirmishers. They were taking no chances on the Italians trying to play possum.

When I rejoined Captain Henry it was after three. The sun had followed the moon in its great arc across the sky but it still hung high. There was no more work for our mortars to do. The men took them apart and the sergeants went out to round up the men who had strayed off. The 155's were still firing over our heads but the shells were bursting a long way from us now and the sounds came only as dull thuds. The stone wall behind which we had crouched in the morning was now something to sit on and hang your legs over the front of, watching the clean-up squads working over the

countryside. From several different directions men were
bringing in little groups of prisoners. The biggest came from
under the very brow of the hill at the narrowest point of the
valley. Everyone exclaimed when they came around the
point for there were several hundred of them in one batch,
and the guards were walking clear of them and holding
tommy guns and rifles at ready. A runner came up and told
us that this group came from the division's headquarters. It
had been taken some hours before but the captors had kept
their prisoners there until the road was clear to bring them
out. After the first few batches, the prisoners had not been
brought up to the command post but were being herded off
to one side of the road below. Eventually, there were fourteen hundred of them.

It was nearly four when the word came for us to go down
to start lifting the mines. We had noticed from the hill where
several of the mine fields were. Where they crossed the
road, it was easy to pick them up for the symmetrical rows
of round holes carved into the hard gravel surface stood out
plainly. D company was to form in the field nearest the
entrance to the valley.

I was half-way down, putting one aching foot in front
of the other, when I came on the first Italian dead. There
were four of them, close together, and the blood that had
run out of them had turned purple and black and dried.
Their faces were wax white. They were infantrymen, and
looking around I could see fifty yards farther down the slope
the tent in which they had lived. They wore overcoats but
neither hats nor helmets. I thought they must have run out
when the attack started and begun climbing up to get at us.
I could not see from where they had been shot but, with
the four so close together, it was probably by an automatic
weapon.

My way led down past their tent. It was a big tent of
light brown canvas and the ground inside was covered with
a thick layer of straw. The soldiers who had killed them had
apparently gone into the Italians' tent looking for others and

had kicked a suitcase upside down. A mess of clothes and papers was scattered on the ground, and face up on top of it had fallen a photograph. It was of one of the dead Italians. In the picture he was dressed like a dandy, in white flannel trousers with a coat pinched in at the waist. His posture was arrogant and strutting. Next to the picture lay a book with the Italian fascist emblem stamped on the cover. The picture must have been taken when both fascism and the soldier who gave his life for it were younger. The end of this fascist's trail was a bed of dirty straw and a dose of the frightfulness he liked so much to impose on others.

Still farther down the hill, I came on an Italian anti-tank gun emplacement. It had been dug almost out of sight into the hard ground and the dirt for the excavation made a little ledge and a parapet. The gun was down behind the parapet, its breech into the side of the mountain. It was sited perfectly to command the road and the approaches to the valley. From the road below it would have been hard to see, harder to hit. The Rangers must have come in on it, as I did, from on top. Along both walls of the hole, where the men who fired it had stood, were boxes of ammunition, open but untouched. The gunners had not been able to fire a shot.

One hundred yards farther and I was on the road. There was no need to send for our mine detectors, for as we reached the road we met another engineer company coming up the highway, the men in front swinging their mine detectors before them. While we had been climbing down, they had advanced through the wire. Behind the men with the detectors, other men were getting the mines out and still farther back they were piling the now dead mines on the side of the road. In another few minutes the road that had been deserted all day would be choked with traffic.

Captain Henry came past, saying, "I'm going back to get the half-tracks. The first trucks that come through here are going to be Stuka bait. Its too damn narrow here. Trucks can't get off the road and the Stukas know it."

The half-tracks were the handiest anti-aircraft protection

we could get. The captain left me with the other lieutenants to keep the men together and to wait further orders from Colonel Chittenden. I looked around. From everything I had read in the book he was dead right about this valley being Stuka bait. On a desert or a plain, vehicles can see dive bombers a long way off and disperse in all directions before the bomber can get set. But in a valley like this we would have to rely on fire power if we were attacked.

Captain Henry was not a man to be niggardly with fire power. He came back with not one but all three half-tracks. And when they had lurched and caterpillared off the road and up onto the narrow shoulders on either side we felt fine and safe. One squad, two squads, a company at a time, the Rangers came down to join us. They lay down on the rocks a little apart from us, made themselves comfortable and went to sleep. They had earned their rest but they were not to get it. They were gone again by the time the Stukas arrived.

7

I TALKED with an old soldier once who had fought in a great many battles. He said that in all his years of war he had never seen man-to-man bayonet fighting. He had seen many charges with bayonets, and had watched machine gunners being bayoneted at their posts, but never a duel with bayonets. Never had he seen opponents so well matched in strength and daring that individual soldiers stood up and fought each other with bare steel.

Bayonet fighting is the most intimate fighting in the war. If ever there might be a perfect balance between offense and defense you would expect to find it in this most primitive conflict. Yet, even with bayonet fighting, it doesn't seem to happen.

With weapons which are lethal at long range there never seems anything remotely resembling a balance of power. If the enemy artillery has bracketed you—that is, if it knows exactly where you are and has fired until it has the exact range and direction of your position—you are then immediately overwhelmed by the force of his explosives. You may be only temporarily overwhelmed and later the enemy battery may be captured or silenced by some other troops on your side, but while the show is going on the contest is wholly unequal.

This seems to be true of a battlefield: that if the battle is stalemated, it is stalemated by the fact that while at many places you are wholly at a disadvantage, at an equal number of places the enemy is wholly at a disadvantage. At each individual spot the men on one side or the other are getting the tar whaled out of them. Thus, as a contest of wills, the battlefield bears no resemblance to a contest of wills between two prize fighters who are so evenly matched that each is able to block and parry the other's blows. Rather it is an arena where scores—perhaps hundreds or thousands—of individual prize fights are going on, in each of which each prize fighter at any given second is engaged in landing a haymaker which seriously damages or completely knocks out his individual opponent. The side that is winning the battle will simply be the side delivering the most individual haymakers.

From dawn until the last of fourteen hundred captives had been brought in at El Guettar, all the haymakers had been delivered by our side. Most of the day there were fourteen hundred Italians versus only four hundred or five hundred Rangers and a handful of engineers. And the Italians had had all the weapons they could handle, plenty of ammunition and were in beautifully prepared defensive positions. The Rangers had simply got the jump on them and nowhere on the battlefield all day had there been any but one-sided encounters.

In the afternoon, when the Stukas attacked us, the individual encounters were just as one-sided—the other way round. At the point of their attack, for all our day of victory on the field, we were as helpless, as thoroughly overpowered, as each individual Italian gun position had been when the Rangers were hunting them down with tommy guns, B.A.R.'s, hand grenades and mortars. Had there happened to be a squadron of allied fighter aircraft in the immediate vicinity, the Stuka engagement would have been just as one-sided the other way round, with the Stukas down in flames and the men on the ground leaping out of their foxholes to shout themselves hoarse with joy.

Almost any modern weapon of war is so lethal that an attack with it, perfectly timed and executed, is devastating—and every single weapon, like each piece on a chess board, can be taken by some other piece. The act of taking, at the

exact time and place on the battlefield, has the finality of removing your opponent's knight from the chess board. The
finality is usually the finality of death and total destruction
or capture. "We" took fourteen hundred Italians off the
board between 6 A.M. and 5 P.M. With equal finality, the
Stukas took a score of Americans and one armored half-track
off the board between five and six in the afternoon, even
though we'd already won the battle as a whole.

On the spot, the process seemed like anything but chess.
The first Stuka attack was several miles away against the
artillery. The Stukas came in pairs and there were no fighter
craft with them. They did not bob and weave as the bombers
had in the morning. They flew much lower, only four or five
hundred feet high, in wide easy sweeps. They crossed the
battlefield and they circled it slowly, looking for targets.
They were a mile or two from where we were on the road
but they were easily identified by the silhouette of their landing wheels. The Stuka's landing gear doesn't retract but remains fixed below the plane and is sheathed in bulky metal
streamlining. On the turns you could see the outline of the
Stukas' wing tips, square and blunt.

After one wide circle over the battlefield, first one Stuka
and then the other rose, climbing steeply until they were
level with the tops of the mountains. And then first one and
then the other made still another turn, tighter and more exact,
swung west towards the sun and then coming out of the sun
dropped sharply. Watching from the road, we could see the
flashes of the bombs exploding.

After the dive, the Stukas seemed to disappear into the
ground and then to rise up out of it again. They flew slowly
away, crossing the battlefield again and disappearing beyond
the hills.

We were too far away to see or hear the gunfire from the
ground. We could see how slowly the Stukas flew compared
to the bombers and the fighters that had come and gone in
the morning. We could not understand why the Stukas had
not been shot down. After the first two, came two more.

Again there was the slow march across the sky and the precise circling maneuver over the target, the banking into the sun and the dropping down, down, down towards the ground. Then there were the flashes of the bombs.

These first attacks came a little after five, and we did not know what damage they had done but only that the attacks had seemed uncontested. We were glad that our half-tracks had come up and were there to guard us.

Just before the Stukas attacked on the other battlefield, orders had come for the Rangers to make one more attack. Four or five miles beyond the narrow part of the funnel there was an Arab town called Bou Hammet. There were still some enemy positions on the edge of this town. The Rangers had filed away to attack them, and Colonel Chittenden had directed us to stay with the half-tracks to protect the roadway from air attack. Now that the mines had been removed and the road was open a steady stream of vehicles moved forward. Wire was going up to forward command posts, and food and ammunition.

The kitchen truck came through and stopped long enough to ladle hot stew from a thermos can as big as a barrel. We had no mess kits with us but the men crowded around and filled and refilled whatever they could find to hold the food— empty C ration cans picked up from the ground, canteen cups, even helmets. There was sliced bread in the truck and I had them pile stew on two pieces of bread and gobbled that. It was grand. All through the day I had chewed or sucked on D ration chocolate bars, or sat and opened one of my cans of C ration and poured the cold contents into my mouth. Now the heat from the stew that was ladled out felt wonderful. And I still had water in my canteen to drink. When two big thermos cans had been emptied, the men in the kitchen truck picked them up and drove on.

The battle was over and we were waiting only for the Rangers to take those last now isolated posts and to come back, and then we'd all be relieved. We knew we would be relieved because the men and vehicles of the infantry combat team were moving through the pass steadily, one unit after another, and they were fresh and had not been in the line all day. They would hold the ground we had taken and prepare its defense against counterattack. Their officers hurried by in jeeps. Some of them had maps and were studying them as they jounced along the road. They were seeking locations for their command posts, telling the signalmen where they wanted their wire, choosing sites for automatic weapons, observation posts, first aid clearing stations and the like.

As far as we were concerned, the show was over. Captain Henry, whom I did not remember even napping during the day, called the platoon lieutenants and me together and said, "They may still find some trouble up ahead. They may want us later. Let the men get some rest."

He said he was going to sleep in one of the half-tracks. The nearest of the half-tracks, to which he went presently, was right alongside the road, on a little bluff five or six feet above it. It looked very formidable up there. Its four machine guns rose above its heavy armored box sides, pointing skyward— the two long black .50-calibres on pedestal mounts and the shorter, slimmer .30's on the sides. The men and the gunners of the half-tracks had been on the march with us and had carried and worked the mortars on the hilltop. They were tired too but they looked alert and businesslike at the guns, their heads tilted back and their eyes steadily on the rims of the hills, waiting and watching.

From where I sat on the opposite side of the road, I was almost on a level with them. The road ran through a cut here and this half-track was protecting its narrowest point. The second half-track was on the same side of the road with me, fifty yards farther in the pass. The third half-track was two or three hundred yards out towards the end of the gap and still higher up the slope, well back from the road. A few feet from me there was the beginning of an ammunition dump, where a passing truck had unloaded a half dozen long gray boxes of rifle and machine gun ammunition.

The two platoon lieutenants had passed Captain Henry's

orders on to the sergeants and now they were stretched out beyond the ammunition dump and were twisting and turning on the hard ground, trying to find a position in which they could relax least uncomfortably. To make the ground flat you had to pry the stones out of it. All around there were men working to make themselves comfortable. If the ground had been sandy they might have dug themselves foxholes, but it was hard and unyielding and, stripped down as they had been for the march, they had no tools with them. They simply spread out and kicked and scratched or rearranged a few rocks and undid their cartridge belts and laid them next to them with their rifles, squirmed and rolled a few seconds and then were asleep.

On the plains the sun was still shining but here in the pass it was already below the rim of the mountains and the wind that was coming through the valley was cold. I began to shiver with fatigue. The trucks and the jeeps came and went along the road and the doughboys filed by on foot and I felt very, very tired. All I wanted in the world was to get out of the wind and be a little warmer and lie still. I took two of the ammunition boxes from the dump and laid them on the ground parallel to each other and to the road. I kicked and lifted the rocks from the ground between them. I went and got a third box and put it across the head of the other two, and then I took off both ammunition belts and took my last can of C ration out of my pocket because it made an uncomfortable lump. I piled all this gear on one of the boxes and got into the bed I had made and lay there.

I lay there with my head towards the wide end of the valley for no particular reason except that that's how I happened to lie down. I felt dull and numb now and I didn't care whether school kept. I took off my helmet and tried it for a pillow but it was too high and cricked my neck. So I sat up wearily to put it back on my head and lying down again propped a small stone under it so that as it rested, my head lay in the leather harness inside the helmet and the helmet itself tilted forward over my forehead and eyes. I had no plan in this except to be comfortable and it was purely accidental that the helmet was so placed. I lay on my back, and I must have gone to sleep instantly and been very deeply asleep when the Stukas came.

Reconstructing it, I know they must have circled overhead, studying the attack, and that as soon as they came in over the hills our guns began firing on them. I know that whistles must have blown and that the infantry that was passing on the road must have scattered, scrambling over the rocks. I know that .50-calibres make a hell of a noise when you are close to them and that in the valley every sound was magnified. But I slept on peacefully through it all and I have no recollection of what finally awakened me.

I only remember sitting suddenly bolt upright and twisting my head up over my shoulder and there it was, coming down at me. It was a Stuka very near the bottom of its dive and it was enormous. I could see its black paint and the lap joints of its wings, and its engine cowling, and the metal pants of its landing wheels. And right down under it, dropping free and clear and seeming absolutely motionless in the sky as I saw them, there were two bombs, one a little ahead of the other, a foot or so apart, absolutely motionless in the air. All this I saw with absolute clarity.

Wholly unmoved, without any process of thought, I saw and knew that the two bombs were going to strike on the other side of the road and not on me. I knew they were going to strike thirty-five or forty feet away and that I was safe from those two bombs and then, instantly, without ordering it, I flattened myself backward to exactly the position in which I had been asleep. My helmet on the same small stone and myself very wide awake, lying absolutely still in the shelter of the ammunition boxes, waiting for the blast.

These reactions were so extremely fast that I very distinctly remember the wait for the explosion—although the wait could not have been more than a second or two at most. The two explosions came exactly as I had seen that they would, in quick succession with one a fraction of a second behind the other. And then what I had not foreseen because I had no idea it was going to happen—just behind the two explosions, there was a third. It was infinitely greater than either of the other two, and infinitely surprising. From somewhere, I knew not where, had come a third explosion, close, almost on top of me.

The third explosion was the end of the world. I can only describe it by saying it was so enormous that it filled the universe and all consciousness. There was nothing in the world but that explosion. There was neither thought nor any other consciousness.

Coming back from that explosion was coming back out of a world in which there had been nothing but the shattering wholeness of it. I was on my feet stumbling. My feet were stumbling and my mind was stumbling. I could not collect myself. I saw my gun on the ground next to me and I reached down and grabbed it senselessly. I ran with my gun, over the rocks, a few steps. And the ground around me came into focus slowly. It was as if I did not know at all where I was and had to find out gradually. I was in a valley and ahead of me the rocky sides were steep and there were crevices in the rock. The first thing I remember wanting was to get into one of the crevices. I went towards it.

A human being came into my new world. He blocked my path. He was a soldier sitting on a rock, his gun across his knees. He looked up at me and his face was contorted and there were tears running down his cheeks. He held something out towards me and he said very clearly, "Please, sir, get them quickly and have them take it off."

What he held out was what was left of his hand. There was no back to it. There were some bones and some red and white patterns, like the patterns in medical textbooks. He said again, plaintively, "Please, have them take it off so I don't have to look at it."

The world came back and back. There was the hand and something had to be done to it. There was a tin thing in a pouch on my belt. There was my general sitting next to me

THE BATTLE IS THE PAY-OFF

By RALPH INGERSOLL

THIS is a new kind of war book — at least for this war—and a revelation as well as a relief for those of us who are crammed with soldiers' narratives which, no matter how exciting and brilliant, are written with little reference to the massive structure of war, in which they are episodes only.

Captain, then Lieutenant Ingersoll, once the brilliant (and controversial) editor of *PM*, has had the experience so common among young Americans in this war. Once in the Army, its life and organization have gripped his whole being and utterly absorbed his interests. And in this book he tells his own story, but only in order to explain and describe from first-hand experience how a modern army operates, how a battle is made and won, and what it is actually like.

The battle, if my figuring is right, was begun and ended within two days. It was the brilliantly prepared and executed flanking movement by which Rangers, assisted by Engineers, climbed the mountains above El Guettar in Tunisia at night, and came down behind the impregnable funnel gorge on the road to Sfax, clearing the way to the Mediterranean in two directions.

Lieutenant Ingersoll, unaware of the coming battle, was

assigned as an observing officer to the Engineers, and almost upon arrival was swept into active work and command.

This is what the book is about, but it is not the book. I can best describe *The Battle Is the Pay-Off* by writing of it as if it were two books, although actually every chapter of the narrative is a skilful blend of what-I-did-and-saw and why-and-how-it-happened. What will be most fresh and informative to readers at home is Ingersoll's skilful and compelling analysis of how a battle is prepared for—which goes back and back in its exposition, until you see how strength or weakness in a training school, or the care of feet, or the combination of discipline with initiative may become, and do become, the decisive factors months later determining win or lose, and live or die. More impressive than his accounts of supply and the location of camps, and the tactics of advance are these dramatic results of right training as he describes them in action, upon which the good or evil fortunes of millions of our boys squarely rest.

I suppose all these things are in the army manuals. But this is not an army manual. It is a vivid, dramatic, scrupulously accurate, and detailed narrative of an army in daring action as seen by one man who shared both the danger and the responsibility. Nothing for civilians who are not to fight themselves will take the place of such a narrative, if written as this one is. Nothing will make them understand, as well as see, feel, and hear a battle, and take their imagination into it in company with human beings who are our own boys.

All the organization behind, the preparation, the morale, the humor, and boredom and tensity of garrison and camp shape themselves like a movie film in this book as Ingersoll moves toward the front. The mine fields are cleared — an operation we hear of every day, but nowhere made so intelligible as in this book. Then the night march begins in dead silence up the rough mountains, the leaders trying to hold the long line from breaking in exhaustion. An officer, then a Ranger, or a mortar-man, or a combat group live for a few moments as personalities—or a "walkie-talkie." Then a perilous sliding descent in half moonlight, first contact with the enemy, sniping, the sudden release of combat by all arms, wounded, prisoners, soon bombs from enemy airplanes and sudden death by your side. At last, clear victory, and you know not only how but why.

Captain Ingersoll is fortunate. He went to this battle as an observer but he was part of it, and so he writes not with the objective summing up of a correspondent, but with the intensity and inner experience of a participant who had to understand or fail or be killed. And yet—as an earlier account of his of wartime England showed—he is also a first-rate correspondent, whose talent is for making the reader see what he sees, know what he knows. And furthermore, his professional military training has opened his eyes to the art and science of war, in which he is presumably not an expert, but to which he comes with the intelligent curiosity of civilian life. His book has a quality of writing we have been hoping for, and seldom getting, in books about the war.

HENRY SEIDEL CANBY

In accordance with a suggestion made by a number of our subscribers, this monthly reprint from the Book-of-the-Month Club *News* is printed in this format so that it can be pasted if desired, to the flyleaf of the book.

PRINTED
IN
U. S. A.

in a plane over the middle of the Atlantic making idle con- versation, playing with a little first aid tin in his hand, saying it was an odd fact that he had carried it through two wars and never opened it. The world kept coming back around me. My belt was on the ammunition box. I got it and I found the first aid tin and tore the metal seal apart and the white bandage fell out. It seemed very large to come out of such a small tin. I picked it up and went back to the hand. The world was still coming back.

There were other men in the world now. They were nearby. They were not moving; they were just standing or sitting or lying still. There was also sound. There was the crashing of gunfire all around, very loud, and through the gunfire, very clearly now, there was the motor of an air- plane. I stood by the hand and I looked up and there were two more black planes circling right over us, going slowly around. They were half way through their circle and they would go over that hill where the sky was still bright with sunlight and turn and then they would come down on us like the others.

I knew now that there had been two the first time and that I had only seen one. The big explosion had come from the other. The hand was not bleeding. There was no back to it but there are no arteries in the back of a hand. The crevice and the man with the hand and the planes overhead all fitted together and I picked him up off the rock, with my one arm around under his other arm and the big bandage still dangling from my free hand. We went twenty or thirty feet, climbing and falling over the rocks and we pressed together against the crevice.

We waited in the crevice for the bombs to come. From where we were we could not see them drop. The crashes of the explosions came in quick succession. The man with the hand made no sound and did not move. He still held the hand in front of him and his eyes were wide and expressionless. I said sharply to him, "Stop looking at it."

I could not get the bandage on, huddling where we were.

The rocks shut us off from the sight of the explosion but I saw the planes going away up the narrow part of the valley, treetop high, framed in the mountains. I led the boy down from the rocks and he sat again, still holding the hand out. It was still not bleeding.

The world continued to come back into focus. I was again conscious of the men close to us, the men who were standing or sitting. There was something the matter with them. They were still standing, still sitting despite the explosions. They had not moved. There was something very much the matter with them. They came into focus like something under water after the water had been disturbed and is quieting again. One man sitting there had only half a leg. One man standing, leaning against a rock, was hugging himself, hugging his chest. Disaster had come to these men. They were all men with hands. My little bandage was a handkerchief in hell. I laid it on the hand and I said, "Sit there!"

Swimming through my thoughts was the thought that I must get help and that there were ambulances and first aid men and doctors on the battlefield. And now the road and the vehicles on it and the plain beyond the road came into my sight. The third of the three half-tracks came into my sight and I saw without wonder that there were sheets of flame rising from it. There was a man in it and he was still shooting a machine gun but the vehicle was on fire, ablaze. Nearer to me, on the road, canted into the gutter, there was a big bright Red Cross on a white background on an ambulance. I went running towards it. There was no firing now but there were other men running and men were calling out. The driver sat at the wheel of the ambulance and he looked pale and sick. I said, "There are a lot of wounded men back there."

He said, "I'm only a driver. I don't know where the other fellow is."

I went down the road the other way. There would be no first aid stations here. I would have to get transportation. All the other vehicles that had been on the road were in the ditch and driverless. I came unexpectedly upon Colonel Chittenden sitting in a gully with a lieutenant next to him. They were looking at a map. Beyond them was a jeep that must have been his, and a driver. From where he sat, he could not see where the bombs had fallen.

I said, "Colonel, I've got a lot of wounded back there and I want help."

He got to his feet and said, "You can have my medical. I have a sergeant and a corporal and they are right here." The sound of his voice was reassuring.

The sergeant and the corporal were beyond the jeep and they came up running when I called. We all three ran back along the road. When we got to the place where the attack had come, the two men who were the Rangers' medical detail went quickly from soldier to soldier, looking at wounds, looking into faces. There was the quiet confidence of the professional in the midst of disaster in the very way they moved.

When the medical men reached the man with the hand, one of the platoon lieutenants was kneeling next to him and he had a sling or his belt or something around the wounded man's arm and was making a tourniquet. He was holding the tourniquet with one hand and feeling on the ground for a stone to put in it with the other. I picked up a stone and handed it to him. I didn't think the wound was bleeding very much. The bandage from my first aid tin was covering the back of the hand but I could suddenly see it through the bandage, the way I had first seen it, and I felt sick and empty.

I said to the lieutenant, "How many are there do you think who need help?"

He went on tightening the tourniquet. His lips were pressed together in a hard line, and he did not answer for a moment. Then he said, "There are some that don't," and went on fussing with the tourniquet.

His words surprised me and I stood up straight and looked about me. There was a man lying limply near us and when the lieutenant saw that I saw the figure he said, "That's Cur-

ran." And then he said, "He was a God-damned good sergeant."

Curran was dead all right but you could see that it was
Curran. The thing beyond him was more extraordinary.
There were the boxes where I had been sleeping and ten or
twelve paces away, at the edge of the little rise of ground,
Curran's body lay. Immediately beyond it there was a gully
shaped like a cup with one side blown out, a cup four or five
feet deep. At the bottom and on one side of the gully there
was a pile of gray shredded fabric. It had no shape and it was
not very big. The whole bottom of the gully was coated
evenly with a gray powder and you would not have noticed
the pile of gray shredded fabric except for a foot and a shoe
with no body attached to it. This object lay by the edge of
the pile.

There was no blood whatever. All the blood had been
blown out of the man who had worn this shoe. He was
shredded and the pile of shreds was coated with the gray dust
of pulverized rock.

The big bomb, the one that had ended the world, had hit
square in the gully where the shredded thing had taken
cover. The force of its explosion had been confined by the
sides of the gully, and had pulverized the rock. The force of
the pulverized rock had been added to the force of the bomb's
shattered steel casing.

The shredded thing was so odd that it was not gruesome.
The two others who had been killed in the gully were not as
badly shattered. You could see that they'd been human beings once.

The medical men from the Rangers' battalion were helping
to carry the wounded to the ambulance which was back on
the road. They filled the ambulance with wounded and it
drove away. One of the two lieutenants who looked alike had
crossed the road and was in the shallow crater the first two
bombs had made. He was stooping. I did not know what to
do next. I began to walk towards him.

It was cold in the valley. I noticed that one of my hands

was all bloody. I thought it was from the wounded man I had helped, but it came from my own finger. All that had happened to me was that a fragment of flying rock had taken the skin off the back of one finger—and scratched my helmet. I hadn't noticed my finger in the confusion.

As I crossed the road, I saw that the half-track that had been hit was still blazing. The gunner was gone. While I was watching, the ammunition in the half-track blew up. It was a terrific explosion and the flames that had been dying down leapt high again. I thought, where do the bullets go when ammunition blows up?

I reached the lieutenant who was still stooping in the bomb crater. He was picking up the metal fragments of the burst bomb. He had four or five pounds of metal in the crook of his other arm. When he realized I was curious he straightened up and I could see that he was very angry. He was panting with anger and his face was as white as the bandage that had been in my kit. He held out an ugly, jagged piece of blue-gray steel.

"You see this," he said. "You see this? I got a place for this. I got a place in a God-damn booby trap for those God-damned bastards."

The booby traps the Germans use are G.I. They are factory made by the loving hands of frauleins. The booby traps the American engineers lay are more often handmade, on the field, from odd scraps of metal wired around a block of explosive and fused so that the enemy who disturbs one will catch the flying steel in the face.

8

THE day after the capture of the funnel beyond El Guettar, my orders took me away from the front. By a curious coincidence, although I was over a hundred miles away, I still had an almost first-hand view of the final phase of the battle. Hitch hiking my way home, about two o'clock in the afternoon I was deposited, musette bag and bedding roll, on the edge of a flying field, just as eighteen B-25 medium bombers were coming back from a flight over the very valley I had left.

News gets around at an airport. Half an hour later I was in the briefing room with the pilots. The intelligence officers seemed fascinated to find a real live foot soldier in their midst, particularly one who had just come from the very spot where they were trying to draw their bomb line on the map. In the air corps, what is called the bomb line is the line beyond which they may safely unload their bombs, certain that they will not hit friendly heads. Sometimes they bomb inside the bomb line when, say, the enemy has broken through. But then it's a ticklish business and the intelligence must be precise.

That afternoon at the B-25 station they had an enormous map on the wall and they had a whole sheaf of printed directions coming to them from forward headquarters by teletype, but they were having some difficulty reconciling the two. Since I had only just left the very hills they were trying to identify they wanted to know everything I could tell them, and I wanted to know everything they could tell me.

It was immediately obvious that something had happened since I left the front the evening before. What happened was that the counterattack that we had been expecting all the time I was in Gafsa and El Guettar was at that very moment being delivered by the Tenth Panzer Division. Our infantry was having trouble stopping it. The air over El Guettar, which had been empty of American planes when I had been there, was now being filled with bomber squadrons. They were going out at two-hour intervals, eighteen to a mission, each mission picking up thirty or forty protective Spitfires on its way forward.

What happened when the Tenth Panzer Division attacked the First American Infantry Division was presently to be written and published in *The New Yorker*, in a profile of General Terry Allen, by *The New Yorker's* correspondent, A. J. Liebling. I had seen Liebling, who is an old acquaintance of mine, at division headquarters on my way out. His account is worth reading.

Liebling describes the terrain in terms of a football stadium, the grandstands being ridges and the playing field the plain between. The bowl he pictures is beyond the pass we took from the Italians—where the funnel widens out just as it empties into the coastal plains. The Tenth Panzer, attacking here, was taking its last chance to destroy the Americans before they could fight their way clear of the hills. Of this attack, Liebling wrote:

At five o'clock the next morning some tanks of the Tenth German Panzer Division appeared on the plain between the two ridges. They had, it was discovered, entered the stadium through gullies in a part of the ridge still held by the Italian infantry, and they began the day by trying to climb a slope and overrun the batteries of American artillery which had been posted below our ridge. Our infantry and gunners stood firm, and our artillery shot through several of the tanks. Tank destroyers, coming to the rescue of the artillery, engaged the tanks, which moved off and started to snake their way down the center of the field toward the western exit. Their apparent intention was to come around the rear of the American position in the north stands and cut the main road back to Gafsa, then retake that town and thus leave Allen's division stranded. If the maneuver had succeeded the entire disposition of the allied forces designed to contain the German army in Tunisia while the Eighth Army smashed its way through the north line might have been upset and the Americans might have had to retreat before the Germans as the Germans retreated before the Eighth Army. The German commander may also have hoped in this way to cause havoc among the cut off American troops and get a great swag of equipment and prisoners. "They thought they could push us over and laugh at us because American troops couldn't stand to German armor," a member of the First Division's G2 said that night after the threat had been averted.

The tanks, snaking their way out of the stadium, nearly ran over Allen's command post, which, fortunately, they didn't know was there. They got within two miles of it, which is close in motorized battle. Our howitzers, firing from their position on our ridge, reached the first element of the westward bound tanks, twenty strong. Four were shot through. Their clumsy black bodies, belching dark smoke, remained on the field right below the command post. The other tanks turned away heavily and scuttled out of howitzer range. The Americans' 105 and 155 howitzers, which are our main field artillery weapon, are not ideal anti-tank guns, because of their arching trajectory, but on that day they served.

Tanks do not rush forward in the mechanized version of the flying wedge, as people at home sometimes imagine. They advance hesitatingly, like diffident fat boys coming across the floor at a party to ask for the next dance, stopping at the slightest excuse, going back, and then coming on again, and always apparently seeking the longest way around. When they do have to cross a plain, they postpone the evil moment as long as possible by clinging to the lower slopes of the nearest ridge until some invisible force pushes them unhappily into the open. When they follow a road, they zigzag in a series of tangents to it, crossing it occasionally and staying on it only when there is no other way through difficult country. They are timid creatures.

All day long, that day of the stadium battle, the German tanks

fiddled about on the field and in the first rows of our grand-
stand while the field artillery shot at them and a battalion of
eighteen American tank destroyers, waddling into action like
bull pups, drew their fire and returned it. Finally, all eighteen
tank destroyers were knocked out, but only after they had
wrecked thirty-one tanks. By the time this tank destroyer battalion was finished, another had arrived from the rear, so our
position was not weakened. During all the fighting, our infantry
stood firm on the hills. Without it, the artillery would have been
overrun. The Tenth Panzer Division made its last effort at five
in the afternoon. Fifteen minutes before, twenty odd Stukas had
bombed our gun positions. The American ground troops had seen
no American planes all day, and the most embarrassed young
man on the battlefield was Captain Fred Kaths, the Air Force
liaison officer attached to the Division. Our air people afterward
explained that they had bombed the German rear positions,
reaching them by a route that avoided the battlefield, but infantrymen like to see their own planes around when they are
fighting. The echo of the Stukas's bombs and of the whistling
devices on the German planes had hardly died down before the
enemy began the attack. This time the Germans sent forward
some armored infantry, known as Panzer grenadiers, whose mission apparently was to climb through our infantry lines and
reach our guns. German tanks followed the grenadiers. American
guns killed all but nine of the approximately two hundred
grenadiers who led the attack, and the rest of the attacking party
stopped and went away. No one knows when a battle is over,
because the enemy, if he withdraws, doesn't tell you whether
he is coming back, but that particular battle ended at that particular moment.

There is one curious reference in Liebling's excellent account and that is the reference to the embarrassment of the
Air Force's liaison officer. I say curious because unless all the
pilots, observers, gunners, and bombardiers of thirty-six
American A-20's and B-25's were off the beam, they spent the
day bombing a plain which was crowded with the supply
vehicles of the Tenth Panzer Division. This was just to the
rear of the attack Liebling describes. I know because I talked
to the crews of each of the last four missions, and with the

intelligence officers we followed their route, road by road, hill by hill. Divisional headquarters, where Liebling was, would not have seen these planes for they skirted Gafsa and El Guettar and came out on the Panzer division's supply train from the far side of the hill mass—but the Air Force's own liaison officer should have known, for somebody from up there was teletyping back directions for the successive waves.

Looking back on it, I am glad I stopped at the bomber station and saw the Air Force at work first hand. Otherwise, I should have come back with the intemperate opinion of an infantryman who has looked in vain for help from the skies when the big bad bombers were coming down. I have no doubt whatever that the Tenth Panzer's supply train made a better target for bombing than its tanks in the field. And I know too that the American planes were sweating their own attack out so fast that they were allowing only twenty minutes on the ground between missions to report, refuel, and refill the bomb racks. None of the crews had any rest from dawn until the last mission came in a half hour after the sun set. I know, too, that the men who were lying in the foxholes, and who manned the anti-tank guns that were destroyed one by one until all eighteen were gone, and who all day did not see any American bombers, must have gone to sleep that night with some bitterness in their hearts on the subject of air support.

There is wonder implicit in Liebling's account as to why the Panzer attack stopped when it did. It had been met man for man on the ground but there was no evidence that the Germans had run clean out of armor. It's a good deal better than possible that the tons of explosives that fell on the vehicles in the rear had something to do with it, for the nearest dumps available to the Germans must have been many miles to the rear. And it doesn't take many gasoline trucks afire to put a crimp in the style of an armored force. There were many fires flickering on the plain when the last B-25's closed their bomb doors and swung home in the dusk.

PART IV

The Battle Is the Pay-off

1

AND now I sit down to write a conclusion. But how can one write a conclusion to a book about a battle while the big battle is still going on? A conclusion makes no sense.

I have left a battle to come back and write this book about it. I did not really come back to write this book; I came back on a military mission. Between jobs, I got some leave—until then I had had only seven days in nearly a year. I spent the time writing this book and my commanding general and the War Department have been gracious enough to let me publish it. But those things do not make me any happier about having written it. This is not, for me, a time for writing.

The story having dammed up inside me, I was able to write this in an incredibly short time—I think under one hundred hours. But already I am unhappy and homesick for the army which is the only place I feel at home now or can feel at home until it is over and the killers that are loose are dead or captured.

Coming back from Africa, I felt it a stroke of enormous good fortune, getting time to write a few pieces about what had been going around in my head on my way home. But I have written a book instead of a few pieces. And I have come to its conclusion and now see how little satisfaction there is in it.

The serious objective of this book was to show the connection between the creating and training of an army—an experience in which the whole of the American people share—and what an army is for: battle itself. Only in battle can the people of the world now impose their collective will on the murderers and plunderers who undertook to impose their will on us.

I have no idea whether I have accomplished my purpose. And I feel that the time I've taken is too long to be away from the war—too long to be talking instead of taking some kind of action, any kind of action, even filing papers.

This is what happens, at least what appears to have happened to me, after a year in the army. I want to write and I don't want to write. I admire my colleagues in journalism more than ever before, I think, since I saw them in action in Africa. I read their dispatches even more avidly than I used to, for they are now writing about places and people I know. But I do not seem to be one of them any longer.

I do not know a correspondent who is a coward. Now and then these men deprecate themselves in their own dispatches. They write that they know they are noncombatants and can never wholly understand or wholly share the feeling of the doughboy in the foxhole. That may be, but it is also written that the correspondents in the theater of action form the only corps that is honestly and completely volunteer. I do not think a pilot in a Stuka can see the white C on the green armband that distinguishes the correspondent, and if he could, I doubt whether he would change his aim. The first great personal loss that I suffered in this war was from the death of a correspondent—Ben Robertson, who drowned in the Tagus River when the Clipper crashed there. He died in line of duty.

I saw many of my former associates in Africa and it was mildly chagrining that most of the times I saw them they were going past me towards the front, going closer to the enemy than where my job stationed me. And going always as volunteers and with enthusiasm and anxious only to get closer, so that they might tell you what it was like there. This is literally true: as a soldier, I had to march behind the enemy lines to get further into action than the correspondents.

The correspondents at the front are brave men and the

correspondents at home—I know this because some of them have talked very intimately with me—are maybe braver still. For not only do many of them fight the same enemy at home that the army fights abroad but in meeting him on the home ground they meet him at his most devious. The fascist at home is just as merciless as the fascist abroad. Fighting civilian journalists and commentators have not even the comfort of a correspondent's uniform. I know the kind of unhappiness this entails. It is irrational, because this great and complex war could not be fought without them. But seeing their friends in uniform, they find it more difficult than most soldiers can imagine.

I know all these things, and writing was my trade, but I do not enjoy writing now. What I think I want to set down, here in this conclusion, is the reason for that.

2

WHEN I came back to America, what startled me most was the new attitude towards the war. I had left after El Alamein but before the Eighth Army had cracked the Mareth Line and before the American army in Tunisia had won even a sizeable skirmish. As I write, it is all over in Tunisia, the Allied Forces have finally and historically vanquished the Afrika Korps and the Americans were in at the kill. So everyone tells me the war is going to be won soon. The optimist tells me it will be over in December. The pessimist tells me it will be over next year. So we are to coast to victory now on momentum—at least that is what they tell me.

It is too late to argue with a feeling that seems so universal. But forgive me if—praying the while that I am a bad prophet—I give you the thoughtful opinion that all this talk is bunk.

I do not believe the war is nearly over.

I do not believe the war will be won by coasting on our momentum.

I do believe the war will be won but not until:

. . . hundreds—not tens—of thousands of Americans, brave, well trained and now alive, have been killed in the process of . . . destroying the armies of the Third Reich in pitched battle on the continent of Europe.

That is why I can get no satisfaction out of writing—simply because I believe there is still so much for the soldier to do, and I am a soldier. It is really just begun, the destruction of the enemies of peace. It is not over, it is hardly begun.

About the war in the Orient I continue to be an optimist, perhaps because I have not been there since it began. I do not believe that when the combined might of the world descends on the Imperial Empire of Japan it can last long. But I do believe that first the armies of the Third Reich must be destroyed.

I cannot leave it at that for if I do it will sound to you like an emotional point of view. It is not. I am emotional about this war but my feeling that the war is really just begun is founded on observation and reason.

This deserves a few paragraphs of explanation.

The most rational prophecies of a short war, without exception, are predicated on the collapse of the Third Reich with its armies still unbeaten. In turn, this prophecy is based on the belief that history will repeat itself, that because the Kaiser's state collapsed before his armies were beaten, Hitler's state will similarly collapse.

This prophecy is usually bolstered by references to the success of our operations in bombing the continent.

In venturing the opinion that the Third Reich will not collapse until its armies are beaten on land, I do not mean to detract from the brilliant air offensive over Europe. It is simply a fact that the continent of Europe is an enormous target and that the most successful raids can do no more than to destroy a small percentage of total production of any one object. I do not contest the military value of this. It is in my belief that Germany's military production may still be rising despite the bombings that I differ with the prophets.

Between 1939 and 1943, the industrial firm of Hitler & Co. expanded its plant to include the foreign plants of Poland, Denmark, Norway, Holland, Belgium and France. Just previous to this, the firm had expanded by incorporating Austria and Czechoslovakia. Coincidental with this expansion, the firm amalgamated with Italy and the several Balkan countries. The underlying concept of all this expansion was the integration of the whole continent of Europe into a single industrial plant, owned and managed by the Germans with subject and captured peoples as the plant's labor pool.

Leaving the problems of running the war to one side, this expansion was one of the most ambitious concepts in the whole history of man. It compares in scale with the industrialization of Russia under the Soviet government. The engineers and managers of this expansion were faced with the problem of integrating hundreds and thousands of plants in a dozen countries. It is wholly reasonable to believe that if the ultimate capacity of this plant is one hundred, its capacity during the early phases of the expansion could not have been more than a fraction of this, from the sheer complexity of the problem.

To give you an idea of what I mean: Technologically, America is a highly advanced country. Yet when it was desirable that American plants manufacture a type of airplane engine that had been perfected in England, the biggest obstacle was the fact that each one of its thousands of parts was a slightly different size and shape from similar parts made here. It was not that we could not machine to as fine a tolerance as the British, it was just that everything was different in the British motor and our machinists would have to learn all over again.

Hundreds of thousands of such problems must have confronted the German engineers and scientists in the integration of the whole continent of Europe into a single industrial plant. If the capacity at the beginning of the expansion was, say, 50 per cent of its ultimate capacity, then in each successive year this capacity would grow—say, to 60 per cent by the next year, to 70 per cent by the year after.

This would be the natural growth in productive capacity due to the integration of the whole plant of Europe under centralized management. The curve would compare to the growth curves of Russian production, when the whole of Russia was integrated under a single industrial management. The comparison is not exact but the parallel is strong. The Germans had the handicap of slave labor to overcome, but

the Russians had an ignorant, non-mechanical people to edu-
cate. And certainly the industrial plant of Europe—the machines and factories available for integration—was infinitely
richer than the plant the Soviet people took over from the
Czars.

If this reasoning is sound, then history will show that the
curve of German production—albeit lowered by sabotage and
bombing—has been going up through the first five years of
the war. (Remember the Russians' successive five-year plans?)
It may still be going up. The lavishness with which Hitler
threw matériel into the lost cause of Tunisia, and the fantastic problem of supplying the whole Russian front through
winter after winter of reverses, confirms my belief that those
who think of the Germans as getting industrially poorer and
poorer may be 180 degrees from the truth.

To this concept of German production, add some tribute
to the perverse ability of Hitler and Goebbels to mislead
their people as to the issues and truths of this war. I believe,
then, that you may arrive at the conviction I have arrived at:
that the German people, now served by millions of slaves, still
think that they can hold out until their enemies weaken, or
are bled to death by submarine warfare or are successfully
tricked into fighting amongst themselves. I believe that the
Germans will continue to think this until the stark truth of
the end of their reign of terror is written by a major defeat
on a battlefield as close to their capital as Waterloo was to
Paris.

So I do not think it is going to be a short war.

It is necessary to emphasize that, and for you to acquire
some of the respect that the American soldier who has fought
one has for an army of the Third Reich. It is not only able
and aggressive; its morale doesn't crack until it is completely
and obviously beaten in the field. If you seriously doubt that,
the dead in Tunisia will arise to haunt you.

The reason I feel that I must emphasize these things is that
I am about to say some other—and very optimistic—things,
and above everything else, I do not want the dazzle of good

news to blind you to the unpleasant realities that we must face.

I do not wish to face the prospect of hundreds of thousands of American casualties any more than you do. But face them I believe we must, for our mortal enemies are still powerful and bloodthirsty. We have still one of the greatest battles in history to fight—for there is no way an army like Hitler's can be beaten except in battle.

And now to talk of good news.

3

THE biggest good news of 1943 is that our striking power is now equal to our enemy's. Three years ago it was feared that there was no possibility of stopping the Stuka-supported Panzer attack on land. A year ago it was known that the German blitz could be stopped but victory over the land blitz was the exception rather than the rule. Victory was usually achieved only with the aid of weather favorable to defense— as mud and snow in Russia. In 1943, a relatively inexperienced American infantry division was able to take the full force of a crack Panzer division's attack and stop it cold. That is news of great significance.

But news of equal significance is that the American armies in Tunisia, thousands of miles from the farms and factories that produced their food, weapons and equipment, were lavishly supplied. The real miracle of the German's fantastic military expansion was the miracle of the supply system that made it possible. There has been a lot of loose talk about how green the American army was in Africa. There was nothing green about the supply system which piled up the dumps at Tebessa and so made victory possible. Hardly more than a year after we entered the war, the U. S. Army's supply system was able to compete as a full grown equal with the greatest military supply system in history.

The underlying reason for this accomplishment, of course, was that the American people did not have to learn about mass distribution and transport from the ground up. We have had a three-thousand-mile wide continent to supply and a hundred and thirty million mouths to feed. We have always done that kind of thing well—whether "we" were the Great Atlantic and Pacific Tea Company, a shoestring truck outfit, or the crews that built New York's skyscrapers. That, however, does not detract from the brilliance of the achievement.

The Germans were foolish to think that young Americans loved life too much to risk it on the battlefield. But Hitler's really suicidal miscalculation was his underestimation of the American people's ability to organize a military supply system—and I use the term "American people" in its very broadest sense because I am thinking at one and the same time of Carl Gray, Jr., the railroad official who was the local American general who ran the railways in North Africa, and of the longshoreman, who is a member of the union that Carl Gray may think is so radical it's subversive. Each in his own job, man for man, either is more than a match for his opposite number in the Reichswehr.

Our allies—the great Red Army and Alexander's men in Africa—mastered the German attack for us and we fight successfully now because we are armed with knowledge of weapons and tactics which they bought for us in blood. But we entered this war already trained to think in terms of thousands of miles and millions of tons, so our supply organization is already the equal of the Reichswehr's. Taking the submarine menace as a constant, there remains, then, only the problem of what is euphemistically called "seasoning" our troops. This is a process not of finding courage—there is enough courage to go round—or of learning the tricks of the trade of killing—men learn quickly on the battlefield. It is simply the process of our troops becoming tough and self-sufficient enough to get themselves quickly to the scene of action and to arrive there in the pink of physical condition.

The principal problem of an army as well supplied as ours is the problem of its physical conditioning and learning to take care of itself on the field. And here is where the battlefield and the training ground meet and are one.

4

THESE are the questions I am asked:

"As a journalist, you visited the British armies and the Russian armies, and you have been with the Chinese. During the years of this war you have been in England three times and Africa twice; you have seen Stalin in Moscow and Chiang Kai-shek in Chungking. Now, you have been a soldier in the American army for a year. How does our army compare with the other armies you have seen, and how does our war effort compare with the war efforts of our allies?"

These questions are not asked so succinctly, but they are asked.

I am now—and I feel it deeply—identified with the Army of the United States, and perhaps I am no longer an objective witness. But I cannot forget what I have seen of other armies nor did I become wholly another person when I put on a uniform.

There are generalizations that come to my mind, and the best founded of them seem to revolve around the word "committed." The officers and men of the armies of which we are allies seem most thoroughly committed to the war, which is not typical of officers and men of our army. This is something that is better understood by them than it is by us. I am sure that many Americans will bring up a host of objections to even the thought that we, as an army, are not committed to the war, wholly and irrevocably.

It is inconceivable that we, as a nation, would accept defeat. It is inconceivable that Franklin Roosevelt has even the shadow of a mental reservation when he restates our objective: unconditional surrender.

The professional officers of our army think only of victories. The individual American soldier is both brave and obedient.

So, if there is a difference between our allies' commitment and our own it is not a difference in kind, simply a difference in quantity and quality. And that is precisely what it seems to me.

Each for his own personal motives, the soldier of the British Empire, the Soviet Union, and Generalissimo Chiang's China seeks the destruction of the enemy for its own sake. The destruction of the enemy is the beginning and the end of his efforts. Nothing else really matters. Although he may gossip for a while about one thing or another, he will always come back to that subject because it is his preoccupation, his obsession, his whole life.

The minute it is put that way, the difference between the soldiers of the British Eighth Army and the soldiers of the American Second Corps becomes immediately apparent. The soldiers of the American Second Corps also seek the destruction of the enemy but they seek it not as an end but as a means. The end they seek is simply to get home. Since it is an end that they seek passionately, they are often moved to feats of great daring to achieve it. But they attack not so much to kill the man opposite because they want him dead as because the enemy stands between them and something they want more than life itself: to get the war the hell over with and to get home.

The American soldier has a battle cry for this. It is: "Let's get on with the job." He is committed to risking his life and to killing simply to get on with the job, to get the war won quickly because only by winning can he get home.

The Russian and the Englishman want to get home as much as he does but they want something even more. They want, they must have, the destruction of our enemy. They must have it because the enemy has made them suffer personally. You can call it revenge if you like but revenge is too petty a word for it. The word revenge makes one think in terms of personal vendettas. The emotions of a man who has felt the evil strength of the Third Reich and the Japanese Empire are too broad and too deep to be enclosed in such a small word. If there is a trouble with the Americans as soldiers, it is the obvious trouble that they do not feel this emotion for they have never felt the force of the Third Reich but have only been told about it. And being told about it is not enough.

There has been a great deal written about the reactions of Americans to their first casualties in battle. With the first dead and wounded came their first experience of personal loss in the war. They were made angry. But I saw no evidence that any felt more than personal anger. To have fired a rifle helplessly at a Stuka that is killing or maiming the men who are your comrades is to have had a moving experience. It is not, however, to have felt the weight of fascism— as the Russians and the British and the Chinese have felt it.

The Americans who have fought on Guadalcanal and in Tunisia are angry because many of their comrades are dead. But they have not lived through eight years of pillage and murder as the Chinese have, or had the richest and finest part of their country taken from them and their wives and children and parents starved and murdered as in Russia. Nor have the cities they love been blown down about them while they stood helpless on the ground, and dug in the rubble for the body of a loved one, as in the British Isles. The soldiers in the American army have had none of these experiences and the amazing tribute to the power of the printed and spoken word is that it has been able to describe and tell them about these things accurately enough to move them at all.

There was an extraordinary respect in the front lines in Tunisia for the men of the British Eighth Army. It was the generous and healthy respect of men who had come to know what war was like and could now recognize when other men were better and braver at it than they. The American soldiers in the Second Corps respected the British in the Eighth Army because they were both fighting in the same desert country against the same enemy. No one had to tell them how tough it was to stop a Panzer attack or to make a successful advance against an entrenched position. They knew now. Watching the British advance on the map, they could translate it in terms of their own experiences.

There is a tendency to hero-worship in the average American and some of the praise for the British was as extravagant as the snobbish, insular, anti-British feeling that many of these same men had probably had only a few months before. The American soldiers in Tunisia were a touch inclined to talk of the soldiers of the Eighth Army as if they were supermen. What they did not understand was the fury that the individual Britisher took into battle, the pent-up fury of years of frustration and defeat, the desperate need to destroy the enemy, to justify himself as a man and to avenge.

The American soldier could not feel for the Russian in the same way—the Russian was simply too far away. Had there been a Russian division in the mountain line in Tunisia they would have felt exactly the same way about its soldiers as they felt about the British. For they were reacting to that kind of deep courage and constant determination that is so characteristic of the Russian soldiers that you cannot eat with them at even a single mess without feeling it.

If it did not profane the memory of the millions who had been killed by the fascists, I would say that the American soldier was learning about fascism the hard way. It is better put, "the slow way," the difficult way of the intelligence and the imagination, rather than the quick and terrible way of the personal experience. For on the battlefield he is meeting fascism at its cleanest. The soldier has only death, disfigurement, or the prison camp to fear from the fascists—not the hopeless suffering of enslavement and the torture and humiliation of those he loved. Neither has he to fear the rape and

ruin of the land that is beautiful and important to him because he grew up in it.

Meeting fascism only on the battlefield, fascism is still an
unreal thing to the American. Since it is unreal to him, he
cannot really hate it. He only hates the man in the ugly black
airplane or the individual he cannot see who is lobbing mortar shells at him from behind the hill. And hating only these,
he is not yet moved by any great desire to root out the cause
of these things and wholly to destroy everything associated
with it—but must fight simply to get them out of his way so
that he can get back home—to a land that has now, in his
memory, grown so lovely that there is no meanness in it, but
only the faces he wants to see and the places where he wants
to walk and the peace there was before all this began.

I am not writing with one private soldier in mind. I am
thinking not only of the enlisted men but also of their officers. Only a few professional soldiers think of the battlefield
solely as a place where professional reputations are made or
unmade. Most officers and men know they are in the war
for the duration and accept that fact, but they do not suffer
because they are being denied a chance to destroy the enemy
when their place in the line is given to another regiment.
They prepare for the invasion of Europe because they have
seen enough of the enemy's army to know that until they
have beaten it in Europe, there will be no victory that will
send them home. When I left Africa they were preparing
with great intensity—because they now also knew that their
lives depended on how well they were prepared. But they
were not planning as men plan to destroy something they
deeply hated. There was no drive which kept them tossing
at night with a burning anxiety to get at the enemy that had
wounded them so. Amongst all the things that were important to them—people and places, freedom and values—the
enemy had as yet harmed them little.

In these things, lie the difference between the American
soldiers and the seasoned soldiers of our allies.

There is the same spiritual difference between the war

efforts of civilians who live in the western hemisphere and those who live in Asia and Europe. This is quite understandable, for the American army, sprung only a few months from the American people, is simply a cross section of the latter. When a British or a Russian army makes a better showing against the fascists than an American, do not be disappointed. Be disappointed, if you must, in yourself. The American army's will to win, whether it be a skirmish or a campaign or the whole war, is neither stronger nor weaker than your own. Although you may not recognize it, you *are* the American army and what you ask of it you will get.

I have been speaking of spiritual forces—morale. Do not be fooled by the flatness of the word "morale" which is the military word describing the spiritual force which moves an army. When there is anything remotely resembling equality of equipment, the spiritual force is the sole deciding factor. My general in the army once listened in silence to a French poilu in Africa who told him that the French could not fight in 1940 because—and he knew because he was one of them—they had been given 1870 rifles to fight with. My general, who commanded a regiment in the line in the last war, heard him in silence and after we had walked away, he said simply, "A man can do a lot of fighting with an 1870 rifle if he wants to."

The line-up of the successful little action I was in at El Guettar was one battery of 88's, twenty or thirty 39-mm. cannon, a score or more of heavy and light machine guns and fourteen hundred men versus five hundred men armed only with the few weapons and the little ammunition they could carry. We won. That phrase you read so many times: "The morale of the Italians is low" was the reason we won so easily. We have enough will to win to beat the Italians. But no man who has seen the will of the Third Reich to destroy and subjugate all the peoples of the world—ourselves at the top of the list—will minimize the quality of the will that it takes to oppose them.

I am speaking of the spiritual force that moves an army,

from its generals to its doughboys. That spiritual force is in your keeping. As the war goes on it is public opinion that will decide whether the prosecution of the war will be even more aggressive—or more cautious. Public opinion will do this inevitably without precise knowledge of the military situation but with that deep emotional wisdom that a people as a whole have—that wisdom on which our faith in democracy is founded.

To one with first-hand knowledge of the evil strength of our enemies, the one thing that is disturbing, about the army as well as about public opinion, is the difficulty Americans still find in facing the finality of this war, which is literally to the death.

Too small a percentage of the soldiers in our army—exactly as too small a proportion of their friends and relatives at home—have in their souls accepted the fact that this is a war for keeps. They are not committed to this war. They are physically committed. They are not spiritually committed yet. The spiritual commitment has been made in the name of the American people by its leaders but the great body of public opinion has not committed itself and the majority of the individuals in the army have not committed themselves. This picture—of our formal commitment and our spiritual lagging—is the exact measure of how far we have gone in the war, and how far we have still to go.

As the battle of Europe progresses, the very size of it, and the inevitable casualties in it, may commit us, as the bombing of London committed the British and the loss of White Russia and the Ukraine committed the Russian people. If so, we will be carried into our commitment on the shoulders of history, just as we have been carried as far as we have gone to date by the historic facts of Pearl Harbor and the submarine war off our coast. But to be carried in that way is expensive in time and blood.

There is only one reason for a soldier to take time off to write articles or a book or to come home to talk to other soldiers or to the people. The reason is to tell them just that.

Our fate as soldiers is in the hands of the people at home, including the soldiers who are still in the training camps. In the determination of the people at home, lie the lives of untold thousands of men.

Every soldier who returns from the battlefield—ask any one of them if you do not believe me—is shocked by the thousand daily evidences of our lack of determination as compared with the determination of our allies. Our streets are full of men and women, young, healthy, well dressed, who play no part in the war. Rationing is a bad joke to men who have eaten with civilians in Chungking or Moscow or London. A soldier does not understand the talk in the papers when he comes back or the crowded restaurants and night clubs where hours of time are as cheap as ten-dollar bills seem to be.

He understands that the men in the factories do not want to be cheated but why is there so much defense of cheating, and so often in his name?

He knows the colossal scale of the American war effort that has fed and clothed him and given him guns and ammunition thousands of miles away. But is it doing these things simply because a few wise leaders have set the wheels in motion or because the people really understand that America is an island in a sea of flame?

It is not a question of settling or stopping arguments between coal miners and coal mine owners, it is not a question of lengthening the training week of the doughboys in camps —or even of shuffling generals faster, bringing the more brilliant and more aggressive to the posts of leadership they deserve. It is not a question of rationally explaining the restrictions that war places on our economy. It is the question of the American people's understanding of the whole war and of that determination which is based only on the kind of understanding the British and the Russians and the Chinese have. When we have their understanding and their determination, the problems that now appear as mountains to the

American people will become, in our new-found sense of proportion, the molehills that they really are.

If the men who are actually in battle do not understand all of this, they have learned enough from the Stukas and the mortars and the mines to know that they at least are committed to a war to the death—that they will not get home until the men who stand in their way are killed or captured and disarmed. If the people at home can only learn that much, it will shorten the war a year and save a hundred thousand lives.

5

THE civilian gasps with sympathy when he hears that his cousin, the trainee, was asked to walk fifteen miles with a pack on his back before he was permitted to stumble back into a nice clean barracks and crawl into cool, white sheets on a bunk with springs in it. One of the most popular songs that has been written about the war commiserates with the civilian who has to make his own bed now that he is in the army. Troops at home complain when there is something the matter with the furnace in the barracks and the temperature is down to sixty. Yet the survival of these same men in the field may depend on whether they are so conditioned to hard marching and to sleeping on the ground that these "hardships" have long since ceased to be any such thing but are simply the wholly natural conditions of life.

It is the practice at home to put troops through rigorous exercises called maneuvers. During these maneuvers soldiers do sleep on the ground and get wet in the rain. But maneuvers are for so many days, for so many weeks, and at the end of them there are the nice warm barracks and the day-rooms and the USO to go back to and in which to sit around and beef about how tough it all was. But after three weeks in the field there will simply be three more weeks of the same and then three more and then three more. . . .

What I am trying to say is that if men are still thinking of this kind of outdoor life as tough, they are not qualified to set their will against the will of men to whom marching twenty miles and sleeping on the ground in the cold rain is the natural order of things.

When men are really well conditioned, living in the field is no hardship at all. When they are hard enough, physically, they understand this.

Then, and not until then, will they be able to stand those short and violent interludes of real hardship seasoned with terror. Those periods will be very short. Neither side could stand them for long. But these are the periods in which battles are won and lost. These moments of violent battle are the showdowns. And they can only be sustained by men who are so tough, so well conditioned emotionally as well as physically, that they will see a nice dry blanket and good hard ground and a mess truck in the morning with hot food for what these things really are in war: not hardships but luxuries.

This is the sense of proportion that the Chinese soldiers have always had and that the Russian soldiers acquired in the first six months of their campaign and that finally came to the British in Cyrenaica. There have been bright and aggressive British leaders before Montgomery—and the brilliant Alexander was in command of British armies when they were defeated. Go back and read how Montgomery won the battle of Cyrenaica: it was in all the papers. He put an army that was already supposed to be veteran through a physical conditioning program that equaled that of the Commandos. And after that the Germans could not stop the Eighth Army. There were other factors but this was the only new one.

This is an odd thing for a soldier who so intensely disliked his own basic training to say, but if I were to pray for a miracle it just might be that every barracks in the United States would burn down. Then the American army in training might start learning to live as it will one day have to live, with the sky for a ceiling and the ground for a floor—in whatever conditions either may be found. An army trained that way would be an army that was at home the day it arrived in the field.

Whether the American army gets training as tough as that—or whether the training even tends to go in that direction—depends one hundred per cent upon you, the American people. It depends wholly upon public opinion. This is why I am terrified at the present wave of optimism in America—because the mothers and the fathers and the older sisters and the brothers will now cringe at the idea of this kind of training. It will seem so unnecessary. Yet that kind of training is the only inoculation they can give to save the lives of those they love. The slightest weakness in battle is instantly translated into death. I have a dent in my own helmet because at the end of only twenty-four hours I did not give a damn how dangerous it was—I was so tired that all I wanted in the world was to go to sleep. I'm not fooling.

The Ranger battalion I marched with at El Guettar had only one casualty all morning simply because their legs were so damn good that after marching all night they had plenty of reserve strength left for their attack—and because they were physically able to attack with such agility, skill, and ferocity that they paralyzed the enemy. It would not have mattered how brave they were—if their feet had failed them they could not have done it. Alone on the mountain top, they would have been cut to pieces by the first counterattack.

Here is one other fact about that particular battalion: *it sustained more casualties in training than it sustained in the first six months of action in Africa.* Think about that!

It is not simply a question of training with live ammunition, although that is important. It is the premium that must be placed on our troops getting used to the living conditions of battle *before* they reach the battlefield. When they arrive, what once seemed hardship to them must be a matter of course and they must have surplus energy. Then that energy, and their whole intelligence and will, may go into opposing the enemy and—if need be—saving their own lives.

The Ranger battalion marched so well because it had only a single 2½-ton truck for transport. Wherever it went, it went on foot, whether it was a single squad on reconnaissance or the whole outfit moving from bivouac to bivouac. The motorized infantry could not compete with the Rangers in endurance marching. Not because the infantry men were not strong and healthy but simply because if you ride in a truck too much of the time, the callouses go from the soles of your feet and the muscles of your legs begin to cramp after marching ten miles instead of not until thirty.

All this is not simply my hobby, although I know it sounds that way. I speak as an attorney for the men over there. They cannot speak for themselves because speaking is not their line of work. But not only have I seen it myself but they have told me often and in detail and with examples. Most of the men I talked with in Tunisia knew I was on a mission and would probably return to the States. Few of them lost the opportunity to send a message home. Nine out of the ten messages that were given to me to bring back concerned training. And throughout all the messages ran the theme: toughen them, toughen them, toughen them.

Many included a second theme: teach them how to use weapons. The day or two of firing on a range that is standard in our training program bears the same relationship to the experience necessary in the forward sector that the two weeks of maneuvering in Tennessee does to the Tunisian campaign. The men in the half-tracks at El Guettar were breathtakingly brave in the way they manned their guns in the face of diving planes. But they were still not good enough shots to bring a single Stuka down. I am absolutely sure that any one of them could have riddled a towed sleeve target on a training ground. They could take their guns apart blindfolded, but marksmen under fire they had yet to become.

I am talking all this time about the kind of training that will save lives and make victory quicker and surer. I am talking about the kind of training that men will think is unfair at the time but for which they will thank God when they get to where they need it. For God's sake, Mr. and Mrs. American People, do not think that the officer who is putting

Johnny through his paces in a training camp is abusing him; he is saving his life—and he is saving your future.

Perhaps I should have written a book about training instead of about a single day's action in Africa. I chose to write about the battle because the battle is the pay-off. It is what training is for. I wanted you to see a battlefield as I saw it and not as you cannot help but imagine it from reading only the citations for heroism in the daily press. It is, first of all, a place where men are tested in their ability to survive—to feed themselves and to keep well, to make and break camp, to know always where they are and to keep in touch with one another. It is a place where physical endurance counts— physical endurance in marching and in waiting. It is a place where skill with weapons counts. For all these contingencies— and they are 90 per cent of any battle—any man can be well prepared. If he is well prepared, he will win and the odds on his being hurt or killed will go way, way down. Men are not in danger twenty-four hours of the day, thirty days a month, but they must be ready for danger when it comes. And their readiness is dependent upon how well organized and in what physical shape they are.

As for the emotional experiences of battle—well, these the soldier gets free.

Battles are like marriages. They have a certain fundamental experience they share in common; they differ infinitely but still they are all alike.

A battle seems to me a conflict of wills to the death in the same way that a marriage of love is the identification of two human beings to the end of the creation of life—as death is the reverse of life, and love of hate. Battles are commitments to cause death as marriages are commitments to create life. Whether, for any individual, either union results in death or the creation of new life, each risks it—and in the risk commits himself.

As the servants of death, battles will always remain horrible. Those who are fascinated by them are being fascinated by death. There is no battle aim worthy of the name except to end all battles. Any other conception is, literally, suicidal. The fascist worship of battle is a suicidal drive, it is love of death instead of life.

In the same idiom, to triumph in battle over the forces which are fighting for death is—again literally—to triumph over death. It is a surgeon's triumph as he cuts a body and bloodies his hands in removing a cancer in order to triumph over the death that is in the body.

These are the thoughts that make it consistent for men who fight for life and hope and love to become hard and to inflict punishment and death on an enemy who stands for death, who is death itself.

In these thoughts I have found my own peace and I return to an army that fights death and cynicism in the name of life and hope. It is a good army. Believe in it.

THE END

Gafsa

MARCH STARTS

MEDITERRANEAN SEA

Algiers
Bougie
Philippeville
Constantine
Bone
Bizerte
Tunis
PANTELLERIA
Sousse
Kairouan
TUNISIA
Tebessa
Kasserine
Sfax
Maknassy
ALGERIA
Gafsa
El Guettar
Gabes
CHOTT DJERID
Mareth
MARETH LINE
Medenine
LIBYA

0   100   200 Miles